A SHORT HISTORY
OF MUSIC

A SHORT HISTORY OF

MUSIC

by ALFRED EINSTEIN

TRANSLATED FROM THE GERMAN

FOURTH AMERICAN EDITION,
REVISED

VINTAGE BOOKS

A DIVISION OF RANDOM HOUSE

New York

PREFACE

THIS CONCISE HISTORY OF MUSIC, which has passed through three editions in Germany and one in Holland, was first produced some thirty years ago. It was written in a few weeks, at a time and place that precluded resort to any books of reference. Lists of names and dates, however, were not my object; my desire was to present a picture of the development of music as a whole, the historical form of that development, and the figures of a few of the great masters. The reader will, I venture to hope, appreciate a certain unity in this presentation, which a mass of details would have destroyed.

The work was originally one of a popular educational series, and as such its scope was very limited. But it never really fitted its frame, for it is not exactly an educational book. It is addressed rather to the reader who has already made himself acquainted with some of the facts of musical history and has heard pre-classical, classical, romantic, and modern music performed— heard it attentively. Of what value to a reader is a history of music unless music is part of his experience? And music of the present as well as of the past. The music of the present explains that of the past, and not the other way round. Of what use to a blind man is a history of art?

None of the later editions of the present book, either in German or in English, is like the first one. I tried to emend and to correct it in every case.

ALFRED EINSTEIN

Note on the TRANSLATION

THE TRANSLATION is the work of several hands. Of the collaborators undernamed some have contributed a few and others many pages. All have undertaken the task as a pleasure for the opportunity it afforded of paying their respects to the esteemed author.

ERIC BLOM

MARIANNE BROOKE

RICHARD CAPELL

H. C. AND HESTER COLLES

EDWARD J. DENT

EDWIN EVANS

A. H. FOX STRANGWAYS

WILLIAM GLOCK

SCOTT GODDARD

P. HOPE-WALLACE

DYNELEY HUSSEY

ROBERT L. JACOBS

MARION M. SCOTT

E. M. VALK

J. A. WESTRUP

BERYL DE ZOETE

CONTENTS

PRIMITIVE MUSIC   3

THE ANCIENT CIVILIZATIONS   6

THE MIDDLE AGES

    THE GREGORIAN CHANT   13
    POLYPHONY   22

THE "RENAISSANCE"

    NEW FORMS   46
    ACCOMPANIED MONODY   63
    INSTRUMENTAL MUSIC IN THE SEVENTEENTH
       CENTURY   84
    PROTESTANT CHURCH MUSIC   98
    BACH   104
    HANDEL   109

MODERN TIMES

    HOMOPHONY   113
    MODERN INSTRUMENTAL MUSIC—HAYDN   118
    MOZART   130
    BEETHOVEN   142
    THE ROMANTIC AGE   149
    ROMANTIC OPERA   161
    OPERA IN THE LATIN COUNTRIES   165
    THE NEW ROMANTICISM   169
    WAGNER   177
    BRAHMS AND BRUCKNER   187
    NATIONAL MUSIC   191

YESTERDAY AND TODAY   194

INDEX   *follows page*   205

PRIMITIVE MUSIC

THE FIRST beginnings of music lie even deeper in historical obscurity than those of speech, the relics of which are very much older. The only means of throwing any light on the subject is afforded by the observation of musical development in children and the music of primitive peoples. To the man who in prehistoric times first perceived musical sound as it originated in the beating of a hollow object or by the swing and whir of a staff, it was something incomprehensible and therefore mysterious and magical. The mere sound of percussion instruments ex-

cited him to the pitch of intoxication. From them he
discovered the power of rhythm, which inflamed
and ordered the ritual dance and also co-ordinated
the movements of labour and, as if by magic, light-
ened toil. At the same time man may have acquired
practice in the use of notes of definite pitch for sig-
nals in war, since they differ markedly from the
ill-defined tones of speech in virtue of their distinctness. From that he may soon have hit upon a preference for the most sonorous and "easy" intervals,
the fourth and fifth. To tone and rhythm was added
primitive melody, in conjunction with more or less
intelligible words, in the first place probably as a
magic initiation-formula of priests in religious rites
or in the song of a chorus-leader in dancing or at
work. At the same time individuals may have been
stimulated to satisfy through musical sounds their
emotional needs, pleasurable or the reverse. A characteristic of the conception of primitive music is
monotony, the endless repetition of the same short
melody, just as the alternation of solo and chorus,
improvisation and a regular refrain are among the
oldest ingredients of musical form.

Natural science has tried to discover a prehuman
origin for music in the song of birds; and comparative musicology, which deals with the prehistoric
development of music, has admitted that primitive
man may have been attracted by bird-song in the
first place and have continued to use it as a model
for imitation. What is certain is that the practice of
music among primitive peoples shows a continual
movement between two opposite extremes, excitement and repose; its typical form is therefore melody that begins on a high note and then sinks or falls
to a definite final or tonic. Attempts have been made
to determine the period at which such melodies

originated on the basis of the range of their musical material—a limited range suggesting an early date, and so on—but without any certainty. Solo and choral song may have existed side by side from the very beginning. Whereas, however, solo song is prepared to take almost any liberties and follows the dictates of freedom—freedom, not mere caprice or absence of rhythm—combined choral singing, whether at work or dancing, presupposes rhythmic unity; and this contrast is found even in primitive music. The combined singing of men and women and the simultaneous sound of voice and some such instruments as the pan-pipes may often have produced at quite an early date a kind of rude, unintentional polyphony —or rather heterophony; that is, arbitrary ornamentation of the same melody by several performers at the same time—and a combination of several rhythms.

THE ANCIENT
CIVILIZATIONS

It is characteristic of primitive melody that the intervals were few, small, and, especially, indefinable and variable. The music of early civilizations is differentiated from the music of nature by the recognition of the octave and all that it involves; by the impulse to tackle theoretically the problem of finding points of emphasis in the tones and semitones into which they divided the scale and, in particular, in its two complements, the fourth and the fifth; and by the consolidation of melody. The pentatonic scale stands as a token of an early stage of this endeavour. This scale is limited to five degrees of the octave, and the less easily compassed semitones are avoided, much as a child avoids and replaces by easier ones the difficult sounds of a language. To this fanciful or expressive use of tones and scales was added actual mathematical measurement, which led to the discovery—beyond the natural divisions of the octave—of mechanical and artificial divisions. These strange, queer systems stand to the natural scales less as rudiments than as degenerations consecrated by convention; and on them were built most refined types of melody which leave us with the impression of an art at once immature and overripe.

The pentatonic or, more accurately, the non-semitonal scale may be accepted as the rudimentary basis of every other tonal system throughout Europe and Asia, and it is recognizable in all the records we possess of primitive music. Of music in ancient Egypt we know too little, in spite of an abundance of pictorial illustrations, to be able to say definitely whether it was adopted in this ancient cradle of culture at the meeting-place of three continents. But in China the development from the non-semitonal to the seven-note scale is certainly traceable, even though the old pentatonic always remained the foundation of its music. In Japan beside the original scale we have a series of peculiar pentatonic scales, in which semitones are employed. In Java the octave is divided into five, or seven, equal degrees, which have no relation to the intervals that we regard as natural.

The musical culture of the Near East is quite different from what may be called in a particular sense "Oriental," that of India and Arabia and Persia. In India the normal seven-note octave is the basis of all melody; but it becomes transformed and overgrown by a whole host of minute intervals employed for

the sake of ornament. The Arabic-Persian system is
even further removed from ours; it is built up of
small units of a third of a tone—originally seventeen and later twenty-four to the octave—and shows
the influence of Greek musical theory. Both these
people have in common a natural disposition for
making music, which is partly mystical and partly
emotional. Both distinguish between solemn, religious
music, which admits the greatest variety in the structure of rhythm and melodies and is frequently independent of speech-rhythm, and music of the folk, in
which melodic restraint is often carried to the point
of rigidity, and the symmetrical grouping of the
smallest melodic units or motives is popular. Both,
also, have astonishingly elaborate instrumental resources, from percussion instruments handled with
great virtuosity to every kind of wind and string
instrument, plucked and bowed. To Arabian music
Europe owes the lute and the violin.

The ancient civilization which has given us supreme examples of the plastic arts acted in music as a
mediator in the most spiritual sense between the traditions of East and West. For the Greeks, too, music
was, as its name implies, a divine discovery. The followers of Orpheus and of Pythagoras still saw in
music a magical means of purification and of heal-
ing. But from the Greek musical practice of early
times to an ideal conception of the art the way was
astonishingly short. They came to regard it as a
necessary element of education and general culture.
They even held it to be one of the pillars of political
morality, believing that the State could no more
than the individual dispense with right harmony and
true rhythm. They placed music among the subjects
in which open artistic competition was held during
the ritual year at festivals, tribal or municipal; and

besides these great occasions there were competitive games; above all, the Pythian games at Delphi, which were specially devoted to music: to the lyric contests, which consisted of the poetical and musical inventions called "nomoi"—the praises of the gods in the definite form of antiphonal melodic strophes, sonatas, as we might say, of pure melody; and, very early, to pure instrumental music. In 586 B.C., actually, the wind-player SAKADAS took the prize with a program symphony on the "aulos" (a reed instrument, not a flute) which purported to represent the fight of the Pythian god with the dragon. But the highest form of this artistic competition was the drama, whose origin is to be sought in the dithyramb, the choral dance in honour of Dionysus. In tragedy and comedy—the union of music, poetry, and dance —the music took the form of solos for the actors and songs and dances for the chorus.

The Greeks recognized two sides to music—revelry, in the sense of elemental excitement, and spiritual uplift. They embodied these in the association and rivalry of music for the aulos, either independently or to give colour to choral song, and vocal music accompanied by the kithara. In the palmy days of tragedy accompanied by the aulos this rivalry was determined in favour of the instrument of revelry; and in this lay the inner meaning of Plato's ban on tragedy. The predominance of instrumental music, the neglect of speech, by which alone man could overmaster the dæmonic element imported by such music, the intrusion of the Eastern conception of music as a merely sensual incitement, the dictatorship of popular taste and mere virtuosity—it was to all this that the philosophic writers ascribed the downfall of the ancient art. We cannot test this judgment of theirs; but it happens that the movement of that downfall coincided with the complete enunciation of the æsthetic of antiquity, with the systems of harmony, rhythm, and acoustics which were to exert the greatest influence on posterity.

The "chromatic" and "enharmonic" of Greek music have nothing to do with the meanings we attach to those words nowadays, nor does their "harmony" imply music in several parts or anything like modern polyphony. The mere facts that tone and words were inseparable and that the musician's time-unit depended on the poet's prosody preclude any thought of ancient polyphony. Greek music was purely monodic. The accompaniment by their favourite kithara, and by the aulos too, did not amount to more than ornamentation of the vocal melody and connecting notes, and occasionally to the playing of certain intervals. Greek "harmony" is a doctrine of melody—of melody so fully and finally developed as to be a convincing refutation of any harmony in our sense. The basis of Greek melody is a scale-theory consisting of tetrachords differentiated by the position of the semitone. These, written in accordance with Greek feeling and theory in descending form, are: Dorian, A, G, F, E; Phrygian, A, G, F♯, E; and Lydian, A, G♯, F♯, E. A further distinction of these elements was made by the three genera: diatonic, A, G, F, E; chromatic, A, F♯, F, E; and enharmonic, A, F, F<, E. Melody so minutely developed as this, bound by fixed laws but susceptible of abundant modulation—that is, combining the various modal species—implies in its hearers an exceptional sensibility for melodic and rhythmic detail; and this in its turn derives from a long and intricate symbolism of interval, with its roots deep in history—from the character (*ethos*) of the different octave-scales. This sensibility is suggested also by the

fact that they were content with the few strings of
the kithara, giving a compass of about eleven notes,
and their weak-toned reed instrument—a very different state of things from ours. The Greeks had no
bowed string instrument and despised the many-
stringed harp of the Egyptians.

The most important of the Greek theoretical
writers on music was the Peripatetic philosopher
ARISTOXENUS OF TARENTUM (c. 320 B.C.), one of the
advocates of the psychological study of music and an
opponent of the speculative researches of the Pythag-
oreans, who were concerned with the science of
acoustics. A compendium of classical theory was supplied by the Alexandrian writer CLAUDIUS PTOLEMÆUS
(second century of our era); but the writers who
actually passed on to the Middle Ages the Greek
conception and doctrine of music were the late
Roman "philosophers" Boethius and Cassiodorus, both
of whom belong to the sixth century. In music, as
in the other arts, the Romans were entirely unpro-
ductive and depended on the Greeks, whom they had
made their subjects.

There have come down to us a few short melodies
of Greek music and fragments of longer ones, though
none of the virtuoso pieces in several sections; and
these we can interpret, thanks to the notation being
in two forms, vocal and instrumental. All these
remnants show how difficult, how impossible it is for
us to recover the expressive value of Greek music.
The Middle Ages and subsequent times knew none
of these discoveries or, if they did, could not decipher
them. That was their good fortune. For the knowledge
of the place music took as an ideal in Greek life, the
marvel of this highly developed system, and the conclusion from these premises that their actual music was

of a unique and exalted character—all this evaluation upon credit has, from the Middle Ages right down to Richard Wagner, had the most fruitful consequences, by blazing up at important crises and stirring men's minds, and all the more since there were no concrete examples of the music itself.

THE MIDDLE AGES

The Gregorian Chant

THE MIDDLE AGES are reckoned in general history to begin with the permanent establishment of a Germanic dominion at the centre of the Roman Empire. In the history of music the most characteristic feature of classical antiquity—monody—survived much longer. It can all the same be fully admitted that a new period of music began with the birth of Christendom. The Faith, or rather the Church, before whose expansive and conquering spiritual might Constantine bowed, while astutely making use of it for his own purposes, had from its inception allowed music an important place in its liturgical exercises; and just as it adopted

foɪ its use contemporary forms of the representative
arts, so it made no difficulty in taking over the
musical tradition inherited from the pre-Christian
world. The source of Christian liturgical song is to be
sought, not at Rome, but in the Eastern provinces of
the Empire. Until the end of the third century, Greek
was the liturgical language of the new faith, and a
relic of it survives in the Kyrie of the Roman Mass.
The Christian ecclesiastical chant was first formulated
at Jerusalem and in the Syrian and Alexandrine com-
munities—particularly in monastic brotherhoods—and
from the beginning Jewish and Greek influences were
inextricably mingled. The incentives from the East,
transmitted and kept alive by Byzantium, remained
more or less active even in later times. It was particularly strong in the eighth century under popes of Syrian
or Greek descent and continued to bear fruit under the
Carolingians in France and Alemannia until brought to
a close about 1050 by the Great Schism. Curiously
enough, the Great Schism also marks the beginning
of the lethargy and decadence of the vocal music of
the Eastern Church, whereas the Western chant begins
only then to bear its choicest blooms and progresses
towards the hitherto unimagined glories of polyphony.

The offices of the Hours are the most ancient por-
tion of the Christian liturgy, the singing of the psalms
having been adopted from the Jewish synagogue.
The actual performance also corresponded to the
Jewish practice of psalmody. It was at first responsorial, consisting, that is to say, of solo-singing by the
precentor, answered by the choir (Cantus respon-
sorius). After the middle of the fourth century
antiphonal singing, which had originated in the Syrian
monasteries, came into general use. As the name indicates, it consisted of the singing of two choirs in

alternation. These were at first contrasted in pitch—
one being composed of men, the other of women or
boys—and later similar. Women seem to have ceased
to take part from a comparatively early date (*c.* 578).

Like the antiphons and responds which were associated with psalm-singing, there are hymns of Hel-
lenistic origin which also belong to the earliest corpus
of Church music. And like the antiphons, the hymns,
too, are said to have been transplanted from the East
into the Western Church by ST. AMBROSE, Bishop of
Milan (d. 397), as representatives of a more popular
mode of song, as the vehicles of a simpler melody.
St. Ambrose took an active part as poet in the making
of these hymns. Like the hymns of the Syrian St.
Ephrem, they are important because of the change
that took place in them from classical quantitative
prosody to modern scansion by accent. Rhyme,
which appeared later, completed this transition. Psalmody, antiphons, responds, and hymns were the
elements that combined to form the complete musical
setting of the liturgy, the form of which was
established by Gregory the Great (d. 604). Doubtless
not without some basis in fact, tradition has it that
the fourteen years of his papacy were crowded with
developments which only later evolution may have
brought to maturity: the collection and standardizing
of the historical musical formulas; the foundation or
restoration in Rome of a song-school entrusted with
the task of preserving and cultivating, in the purity of
its tradition, the wealth of liturgical song. From this
establishment was to ensue the dissemination throughout the entire Christian world of the authentic antiphonal. It was very soon carried to Ireland and later
into the vast Frankish Empire. It was often modified
or simplified, but always restored. In fact, in course
of time other "dialects," so to speak, of ecclesiastical

song—the Gallican, for instance, in the Western Frankish kingdom, and the Spanish (that is, Mozarabic)—had to give way before the Roman; and only the Ambrosian preserved its minute and no longer clearly definable particularities.

Western church music, or Gregorian song, was bound up with a uniform cult-language, Latin. The church song of the Eastern Roman Empire was without this bond. It consisted of religious poetry and music, which had grown up on national soil and consequently remained split up into a number of musical "dialects," such as the Syrian, the Byzantine, and the Armenian; and though these dialects were related, they were individually distinguished by the regions to which they belonged. Later came Russian church song, trailing in the rear of these developments; indeed, it might be described as a bastard child of Eastern church music, since not only "Greek" (or Byzantine) but also Slavonic blood flowed in its veins. In Byzantine church music the development of the "tropes"—short verses interpolated between the verses of the psalms—led to the creation of hymns, strophic poems, often of great length, which later, possibly in the seventh century, developed into the stricter and more elaborate "canons," as they were called. It was not till the tenth century that definite limits were set to the use of this rich store of poetry and melody in the liturgy, with the result that the poetical, though not the musical, development of the Byzantine hymn came to an end.

The contrasting styles of responsorial and antiphonal singing shaped the liturgical music of the whole of the Middle Ages, which derived its artistic life from them. Choral singing was by its very nature the vehicle of a simple, syllabic music and the representative of tradition, whereas solo-singing, with its delight in

melismatic ornamentation, naturally challenged tradition and became the organ of progress. Singers who
appeared to forget the impregnability of liturgical
song might attempt to transform it, but in spite of
them responsorial song continued to gain ground. It
had its stronghold in the Mass, which, though all its
details were not finally determined until the eleventh
century, slowly rose to be the most richly equipped
central element of the liturgy and took precedence
over the offices of the Hours. And in the Church,
congregational singing has tended to become restricted
in favour of performance by a class of specially trained
singers.

Solo-singing has indeed always had to deal with
certain conflicting claims—between verbal stress and
metrical accent and between pure melodic expression
and declamation. Already St. Augustine was suspicious
of the effect of richly melodic ornamentation. A particularly debatable field was the wordless Jubilus, the
Alleluia-singing which Pope Damasus (d. 384) had
introduced to the West from Jerusalem and which
supplied the foundation of those curious interpolated
songs, suggested by a Byzantine model, which from
the ninth century were cultivated under the name of
"proses" or "sequences" in the monasteries of western
Europe. The melismatic extension of the Alleluia was
replaced by texts syllabically adapted to definite poetic
forms suitable for antiphonal singing. Perhaps the piety
of the monks had been offended by the luxuriance of
the melismatic element, or the object may have been
to give a definite rhythmical construction to melodies
otherwise difficult to remember; or possibly pious
fervour demanded that the nature of a particular office
or liturgy should be emphasized. The same spirit also
gave rise to the tropes—syllabic interpolations orna-
menting the music of the Mass. The principal author

of sequences was NOTKER BALBULUS (d. 912), a monk
of St. Gall, to whom the text of the antiphon *Media
in vita in morte sumus* was for long erroneously at-
tributed. Among his followers were Waltramus, Wipo,
Berno von Reichenau, and Hermann the Lame. TUO-
TILO, author of tropes, was his contemporary and also
lived at St. Gall. We shall see that in these syllabic
interpolations, which took the place of the Oriental
melismata, lay the seed of polyphony—the seed, too,
of the liturgical drama, since many of these tropes,
those for Christmas and Easter, for example, were
treated as dramatic dialogues with question and answer. The popular tendency which the sequences revealed during their first rise in Alemannia soon gained
strength, and the later sequence poems, such as those
of ADAM DE ST. VICTOR (eleventh century), the *Dies
iræ* of THOMAS DE CELANO, incorporated in the Requiem Mass, the magnificent *Stabat Mater*, probably
by JACOPONE DA TODI (both of these dating from the
thirteenth century), are, in both their literary and
their musical form, popular hymns.

In spite of all subjective movements, Gregorian song
has on the whole exhibited a remarkable constancy;
and the Church was right in exercising over music in
this instance an artistic control which it never again,
and in no other field, insisted upon with the same
obstinacy. The vitality, ever effective and ever renewed, of Gregorian melody is based upon its simplicity and purity; upon its melodic severity, by which
it may also have differentiated itself from the melodic
expression of pagan Rome, since the regularization of
its melodic progress rests upon a simplification of the
classical theory of melody; upon the distinguishing of
four "authentic modes," the first D, E, F, G, A, the
second E, F, G, A, B, the third F, G, A, B, C, the
fourth G, A, B, C, D, with which the four "plagal

modes" are connected by completion of the lower octave. Of these eight modes the authentic are to be regarded as a combination of the intervals of the fifth and fourth (D, A, D, etc.), the plagal as a combination of the fourth and fifth (A, D, A, etc.). The former create a feeling of rest and stability; in the latter there is a striving to come to rest. In mediæval theory they were given, inaccurately, the names of the classical scales. Together with these designations they acquired the definite ethical attributes which each of those scales was supposed to possess. These associations held good until the disappearance of the church modes and furnished important indications of the significance they expressed. Within these modes melodic formulas of Gregorian song were developed, and the distinct character of each mode is as evident from the preliminary intonation and final cadence as from the note chosen for the recitation. The typical Gregorian melody begins with the intonation, consisting of a definite formula, which rises to the monotone or reciting note; it remains on that note for a time and then descends again with a formal cadence. Though Gregorian song is necessarily restricted, there are numerous gradations of structure between the simple syllabic setting and the florid melismatic type, and to these it owes its abundance of forms, from the simplest song-melody to an elaborate organization that suggests comparison with the later sonata.

The early Middle Ages made a comprehensive study of the theoretical treatment of plainsong. The most complete formulation of principles was achieved in the eleventh century at the Reichenau Monastery in the writings of HERMANN THE LAME. Classical conceptions naturally played a large part in the establishment of theory. The most important of those who helped in the transmission of the legacy was, as I have

already mentioned, the late Roman philosopher BOE-
THIUS (d. 526); from him was derived the conception
of music that dominated the whole of the Middle
Ages. Creative power was ranked below theoretical
knowledge; and though this attitude helped to give
music its place in the scholastic culture of the time, it
was bound to introduce into living creation a strain
of purely abstract artificiality.

The notation used for the Gregorian plainsong—
that of the neumes—was vastly superior to the Greek
system. Its function was to call to mind a comparatively small number of familiar types of melody. For
that reason the exact definition of Greek notation was
abandoned. The music being purely vocal, the notation
dispensed with indications of rhythm; but it possessed
an immediate intelligibility that was lacking in the
Greek system, since it actually gave a visual representation of the rise and fall of the melody. It became
the sure foundation on which modern notation was to
be built; the one thing it lacked—the exact indication
of intervals—was supplied by GUIDO D'AREZZO in the
eleventh century. Anxious as he was to arrest the decay that was threatening the survival of church song,
Guido hit on the simple but inspired device of fixing
the pitch of the notes by means of lines a third apart.
The non-representational system of letters and figures
remained in force right down to the eighteenth century, but only for instrumental music—a quaint para-
dox, since the lines of the staff are actually nothing
but the direct representation on paper of the strings of
an instrument. Guido's "solmization" also provided the
theoretical basis for a more fully developed system of
composition. Thus at a time when music was still confined to monody the ground was already prepared for
harmonic relations and the principle of transposition

and modulation (or "mutation"); and this system remained in force for the next five hundred years.

Solmization is an extension of the classical theory of scales, in so far as it shows the relationships of notes—that is, the distinct position of the semitone in the scale—not in the tetrachord (series of four notes), but in the hexachord (series of six notes). The doctrine of solmization makes use of definite names for the notes—do, re, mi, fa, sol, la (whence the name "solmization"), and so at the same time indicates their individual functions. The three six-note scales, starting from what we call C, G, and F (the last with the fourth note of the scale flattened), all exhibit exactly the same relationships of tones and semitones and so all begin with "do." Modulation (or "mutation") always means that a note has changed its function in the scale, and with the change of function it naturally changes its name as well. Our modern methods of indicating notes by words, such as tonic sol-fa, are simply adaptations of solmization to our system of octaves, with its more extensive opportunities for modulation. Guido's complete scale consisted of twenty notes, from G on the first line of the modern bass staff to E on the fourth space of the treble. As an aid to learning it, students were given a memory-line which was in a literal sense "handy." It began at the extremity of the thumb and ran more or less in the form of a spiral over all the joints and tips of the fingers; it was known as the "Guidonian Hand." It was not till the beginning of the eighteenth century that this system received its actual death-blow (from Mattheson); but in practice it had disappeared much earlier, when the church modes gradually gave place to the establishment of the major and minor modes, as the normal constituents of tonality, about the year 1600.

Polyphony

When Gregorian plainsong was at its height, the
most important event in the whole of Western musical
history occurred: the birth of polyphony. This was
nothing less than the beginning of that development
of an art based on laws of part-writing and harmony
to which we remain subject at the present day. The
ancient world had, of course, often stumbled on the
fact of harmonic consonance. The achievement of
the Middle Ages was that men did not rest content with
that fact, but used it to cultivate a seed that was to
grow to a new and immeasurable harvest.

Rousseau called polyphony "a Gothic and barbarous
invention." He was right in a deeper sense than he
realized. The pleasure in harmonic consonance is
indigenous to the folk-music of the Northern races.
We do not know whether the "lurs"—similarly voiced
bronze horns for calling to the assembly, constantly
found in pairs and dating from long before the time
of Julius Cæsar—emitted a two-part signal blast to the
Germanic peoples on the Western shores of the Baltic.
It is certain that the Irish philosopher JOHANNES
SCOTUS ERIGENA, about the middle of the ninth century, understood two-part singing (probably the An-
glo-Saxon Aldhelm at the end of the seventh century
already refers to it). If we may trust modern research,
it seems not impossible that other European countries
also knew polyphony in the early Middle Ages. All
our actual evidence, however, comes from the British

Isles. Here at the end of the twelfth century GI-
RALDUS CAMBRENSIS mentions a long-standing practice
of popular part-singing, transmitted from father to
son, in Wales and northern England and considers
that it was transplanted there from Denmark and
Norway. Further, for the first time we meet in the
Celtic crwth with a bowed string instrument (already
attested in 609) the essence of which is the simultaneous sound of one string bringing out the melody
against the harmony of the drone strings. Performance
on this instrument must have led quite early to a
selection of the more attractive harmonies. Akin to the
crwth were various other instruments—the most perfect was the vielle—which maintained their hold on
popular favour throughout the Middle Ages. The
members of the viol family were their heirs, and the
modern violin their grandchild.

The development of polyphony depended in large
measure on the theoretical writings of the churchmen.
Or, perhaps one might say, the higher culture of the
period continually acquired fresh stimulus from sources
unknown to us and developed that stimulus still further on its own lines. Frequently the source is still
traceable, as in the famous canon *Sumer is icumen in*
by the Monk of Reading [?] (*circa* 1300), the monu-
ment of a folk-art of unforced imitation, of which the
continuation does not appear till half a century later.
It may be a mere chance that in the widespread
development along similar lines, first France, then Italy,
then suddenly England again came to the fore, till in
the middle of the fifteenth century the "Netherlanders" (northern French, Flemish, and German composers are included under this name) assumed an
undisputed world-power in music.

The first application of theory to polyphony is the
famous description of "organum" in the treatise en-

titled *Musica Enchiriadis*, which was for long attrib-
uted to HUCBALD (*c.* 840–930). This seems to indicate
that both in the North and in the South an actual
practice—the improvisation of a higher subsidiary part
to a given melody—had become stereotyped into a
rigid theoretical formula; that is, the addition of one
or more subsidiary parts to a liturgical melody at
distances of a perfect fourth and fifth. The same
treatise, however, also gives instruction in another
kind of polyphony, known as "free organum," in
which the added part does not follow the given
melody in strictly parallel motion. We find polyphony
also described by the Greek word "diaphony" and
later by its Latin equivalent, "discantus."

In the course of time simple descant, which was
unwilling to move more than a fifth away from the
"cantus firmus" (as the principal melody was called),
very soon learned to assign to the interval of a third
the place which theoretical harmony still denied it,
and came to realize the value of contrary motion as
well as the parallel movement of the parts. The English gymel in two or three parts, which later crossed
over to the Continent as faux-bourdon, corresponded
to the French practice of "déchant" cultivated at
Notre Dame in Paris. It was a form of improvisation,
in which the subsidiary parts moved in parallel thirds
and sixths with the "cantus firmus."

It is astonishing that, in spite of the improvisatory
character of this church music written for voices only,
a considerable number of actual records should have
survived. Thus from the eleventh century, at the end
of which music took a great step forward in France,
we have the so-called Winchester Tropes, containing
over a hundred and fifty "organa" or pieces for the
Mass and the Office, which are characteristically
written still in neumes, so that the intervals between

the parts are not clear. But manuscripts in line notation
dating from the twelfth century give us examples of
note-against-note compositions in which the duplum,
or upper part, already has a more independent
movement. From this it is only a step to the work of
the Paris school of Notre Dame, the principal record
of which is a manuscript at Florence dating from the
middle of the thirteenth century.

At the end of the twelfth century Paris became the
main centre for polyphonic music. Here we meet
already the names of two typical composers: the
elder, MAÎTRE LÉONIN (after 1150), and the younger,
Pérotin "le Grand," who reached the height of his
creative activity about 1220. In mentioning these names
we should remember that the position occupied by
musicians in the Middle Ages was fundamentally different from that of the modern "artist." The mediæval
musician's life was bounded by the culture of the
Church. This was the circle in which he moved and
worked; and only if he was a man of genuinely
creative gifts did he rise from the position of an
anonymous craftsman to the full glory of independence and fame. Léonin worked at his organa as a
goldsmith at some fine ornament. He produced a
cycle of compositions for the whole of the Church's
year, including responses, graduals, and alleluias in
the polyphonic style (he did not touch the rest of the
liturgy), and called his work or allowed it to be called
Magnus Liber organi de graduali et antiphonario. For
the first time we have a strong contrast between the
rigid plainsong tenor and the decorative melismata that
move above it. In fact, the upper part has driven the
tenor into comparative obscurity in the background.
The "descant" parts of this *Magnus Liber* were re-
modelled by Pérotin; he shortened or expanded them,
introduced further melodic elaboration, and gave the

upper parts a livelier and more "wordly" character. But much of it he left unaltered; he had no interest in the production of an individual work of art. Three- and four-part organa by him have also been preserved.

All these forms belong to the most primitive stage of polyphony; but it was not long before improvisation was accompanied by the appearance of a further development in the art. This may be called "poly-melody," the compulsory combination of two or more distinct melodies with different rhythms and, indeed —what was a most remarkable custom—with texts that were not only different but actually in different languages. The root of this remarkable custom lay in the importance of the trope, so significant a feature of the spirit and art of the Middle Ages. In the past the trope had been merely an interpolation in the liturgical chant; but from the twelfth century it was used as a subsidiary part above the liturgical theme in the tenor, to which it supplied an appropriate inter-pretation, the two parts being heard simultaneously. Such a combination of several melodies naturally became possible only when the principle of time had previously been established and the nature of con-sonance and dissonance understood. Among the theo-rists who accomplished this task was the famous FRANCO OF COLOGNE, who perfected the principle of triple time. The principle form of this primitive yet artistic "polymelody" was the motet, which in some cases combined one or even several secular songs with a liturgical tenor. "Motet" was the name given to the part with a new text over the given tenor; over the motet a third part might be placed (triplum), over that a fourth (quadruplum). But in the thirteenth century the favourite practice was to rest content with the triplum; a fragment of plainsong served as a bass, presumably for instruments, and with this were com-

bined two church paraphrases or, more often, two
secular songs with French texts.

The decisive step from organum to the motet was
marked by the textual, as also the musical, independence of the upper part, or duplum. This accounts
for the term "motet," the text of the upper part being
an extension of the "mot" of the tenor. The real difference between a three-part organum and a three-
part motet is that in the former the two upper parts
are twin melodies, while in the motet the triplum is
independent of its companion. There is little question
here of free composition, of "creation" in the modern
sense of the word; it is an art rather of combination,
and this is evident from the numerous ways in which
melodies could be combined, as shown in the manuscripts that have been preserved. The same tenor is
often accompanied by several dupla, and the same
duplum by different tripla. Invention had no part in
the spirit of the Middle Ages. The given material was
treated with protective care and reverence; it could be
used, but not rejected. As Friedrich Ludwig says, "the
repertory of tenors used in the *Magnus Liber* remained
for a long time practically the only source for the
tenors of the French motets." The most curious
feature of this form of polyphony was the ingenuous
combination of sacred and secular, of liturgical and
profane, the arbitrary union—as it seems to us—of
incompatible elements. This practice is the result of
the fact—noticeable quite early in the motet—that
less and less notice was taken of the connexion
between the texts of the tenor and duplum. This
cheerful unconcern grew until it reached the point
where an actual delight was taken in bringing together
the most violent contrasts in a single piece. How did
this come about? The answer is that in the meantime
a secular art, an art of the laity, had been developed

to the highest degree of independence, and the church and monastery were no longer the only places where music was cultivated.

From the eleventh century there had existed side by side with the Gregorian chant a secular art of song belonging to the upper classes of civilized society—the art of the Provençal troubadours and the northern French trouvères. Poetry and music were here fused in an inseparable unity. In spirit their art derived from the popular music of the wandering minstrels (descendants of the mimes and "histriones" of the Roman Empire), and the ideals of the period of the Crusades supplied it with new sources of inspiration; but it borrowed its actual form from the monastic sequence. Of the monasteries that cultivated the trope and sequence with loving care and made possible the communication of their treasures to secular art, the most important, apart from St. Gall, was ST. MARTIAL DE LIMOGES; and it was from the neighbourhood of Limoges that the first and most distinguished of the troubadours came. The art of the troubadours began originally with religious stanzas and then turned to subjects and forms of expression which stirred the lofty temper and knightly fancy of the nobles: courtly love, politics and morals (in the "sirvents"), dialogues of the most diverse kinds ("tensos"), disputations (the "jeu-parti"), laments for the death of a nobleman, topical songs, and finally the form related to the sequence—the "lai." Beside this repertory for the castle there grew up that for the village: dances and maying-songs ("estampidos"), rondeaux and pastourelles. The epics ("chansons de geste") belong to both spheres.

Just as the germ of the sacred drama lay in the antiphonal scheme of the sequence and in the trope, as soon as it lighted on the appropriate material—such as the conversation of the three Marys hastening to the tomb, the brama of the Wise and Foolish Virgins, and the Daniel story—so the secular drama developed out of the dance-song. These first dramatic pastourelles display their folk-character in that they are seldom without some sarcastic reference to the courtly classes. To the jongleur fell the task of presenting the music, of giving formal shape to the tunes which his master invented; and it is extraordinary how successful he was in finding the musical solution of the problems of form presented by the varied, elaborately organized, and even over-refined strophic structure of the poet, and with what subtlety he observed the construction of the strophe, the indications of rhyme, the repetitions of part of the strophe, and the relation of the strophe to the refrain.

The text of a large number of songs by the Provençal poets, the troubadours, has been preserved, but unfortunately only a few—just over 250—of the melodies have survived. Those of the most famous of them, BERTRAN DE BORN, have practically all disappeared. We are much more fortunate with the melodies of the trouvères, of which we possess several hundred, in many cases more than one tune to the same poem. Four generations of trouvères are reckoned during the period from the end of the twelfth to the end of the thirteenth century. COUNT THIBAUT of Champagne, King of Navarre, was the most prolific representative of the third generation; in the fourth we can see the first signs of the change from the aristocracy to the middle classes.

Unlike Provence and northern France, Spain and Italy produced practically nothing but single-voice settings of poems of a sacred or spiritual character. In Spain the principle and indeed almost the only work of this kind is the song-cycle in praise of the

Virgin written by King ALFONSO X, OF CASTILE,
surnamed "el Sabio" (the Wise), who reigned from
1252 to 1284, and provided with a number of older
melodies which, according to Spanish scholars, are
derived from Mauro-Andalusian dances. In Italy a
new type of sacred song owed its origin to the influence of that great saint FRANCIS OF ASSISI (1182–
1226), who was canonized two years after his death.
The extent of his influence may be realized by re-
membering that fifty years after his first foundation
there were already eight thousand Franciscan houses
all over Europe. This amazing man broke down the
Church's privileged right to sing God's praises and
enabled the laity to create their own hymns. A new
source of inspired popular religious song came into
existence—the "laude," congregational hymns for domestic devotions, flagellants' pilgrimages and proces-
sions, the melodies of which scarcely changed their
character at all until the beginning of the seventeenth
century. Before long these hymns adopted dialogue
form and so eventually gave birth to the later oratorio;
but until about 1400 they remained strictly single-
voice settings.

As at the height of the courtly art the jongleur
played the most important part in the discovery of
the musical side of it, so after its decay the ballad-
singer or mendicant musician was active in the dissemination of the secular music of the Middle Ages.
Thence proceeded that treasure of song-melody which,
side by side with the Gregorian chant, but approximating more nearly by a natural growth to our major
and minor tonalities, became the melodic kernel of all
the ecclesiastical and secular music of the following
centuries. The tensos and sirventes of the trouvères,
together with the topical songs of the German Minnesänger, entered on their long winter sleep in the

miniature-bedecked manuscripts, while popular tunes were beginning to permeate the whole of polyphonic music with a living force.

The melodies of the Minnesänger were first noted down at a time when they were no longer to be heard from the lips of their creators. Of all the great collections of songs mentioned in histories of literature, only two contain melodies; the first is the Jena Manuscript, dating from the end of the fourteenth century, which contain 91 tunes, and the second, the so-called "Colmar" Manuscript, which has 107—making a total of 196 (two being common to both collections). There are also a few further pieces, the most beautiful of which are those by the popular singer NEIDHART VON REUENTHAL. In the songs by the Monk of Salzburg, contained in the Mondsee-Wiener Manuscript, there are already some bits of rude polyphony. Only a few decades ago the discovery of the "Münster fragment" gave us a few more melodies by WALTHER VON DER VOGELWEIDE, the finest German song-writer of the Middle Ages. A late follower of the Minnesänger was the South Tyrolese composer COUNT OSWALD VON WOLKEN-STEIN (d. 1445), who also made some experiments in part-writing.

The middle-class art of the Meistersinger, a survival of the "Minnegesang," continued for a longer period as a thing worthy of respect but always becoming spiritually drier and musically impotent, a mixture of devotional and secular song but not an organic compound. In these songs the relationship between word and sound, between text and melody, became changed. New texts were written to given melodies; but the tunes themselves were often prolonged to such an impossible length with a mass of ornaments—"Blumen" (flowers), as they were called

—that it is very difficult to recognize their original shape, and the poems were limited to didactic and moralizing themes. However, among the many schools of South and central Germany there were one or two prominent Meistersinger who are not to be despised as melodists, such as the Swabian weaver MICHEL BEHEIM in the fifteenth century and the Nuremberg shoemaker-poet HANS SACHS in the sixteenth. The richest collection of Meistersinger tunes (334 "Tone" or tones) is preserved in Adam Puschmann's great song-book, dating from 1584.

It is no mere coincidence that among the motet-composers of the thirteenth century we find a few trouvères, one of whom, ADAM DE LA HALE, became with his *Jeu de Robin et de Marion* the ancestor of all dramatic poet-composers. The motet, originally an embellishment of divine service, but forgetting more and more the consideration of that purpose, pursued a course further and further in the direction of secularity. The liturgical tenors were replaced by secular song-tunes or, at all events, were converted into merely instrumental basses. When in the year 1324 a papal bull laid down stringent regulations against the increasing misuse of polyphony in the Church, the "New Art" was based almost entirely on a middle-class secularity, and continued so for a long time, at least in Italy. "Ars nova" was the name taken by the music of the early fourteenth century in contrast to "Ars antiqua," the motet style of the previous century, principally because it added the doctrine of duple time to the triple time which the "Ars antiqua" regarded as the only road to salvation, and at the same time brought about an extraordinary refinement of notation—the development of an abstract theory of time-measurement, which finally freed polyphony from dependence on a text, and hence on the singing voice, and gave it wings of its own. With the "Ars nova" arrived the possibility of an independent polyphonic instrumental art.

The name "Ars nova" was given to this new art about 1325 by the Bishop of Meaux, PHILIPPE DE VITRY (1291–1361), well known as a musician and poet, who also began to strike out new paths as a "composer." The most remarkable evidence of the change in notation is furnished by the celebrated Montpellier Manuscript. This contains a collection of notes, examples of the old and of the new style being preserved in separate sections; so that in the same manuscript we find both the old or modal notation and also the new or mensural; here the change from the quadrangular to mensural notation is quite plainly marked. There now began a time of endless confusion in notation, which was not cleared up till nearly a century later. About the time of Dante's prime (c. 1300), when the Western world received through him its first great poetry in the vernacular, there arose in PIERRE DE LA CROIX of Amiens the first man to make a modest attempt at establishing a new system of rhythm by inventing the smaller note-values. The contrast between long and short notes became more sharply defined as the difference between them became greater, and the vocal character of the art of polyphony changed in favour of the possibilities and tendencies of an instrumental style. The whole art became "humanized." It escaped from the narrow bondage of the Church; the gradual replacement of Latin by French tenors is one of the signs of change. Creative personality made its appearance on an entirely new level of individual craftsmanship. North of the Alps the fourteenth century was the age of GUILLAUME DE MACHAUT, south of the Apennines that of FRANCESCO LANDINO.

Machaut was born in Champagne. He was for many years in the service of the warrior King John of Bohemia and later enjoyed the patronage of the French court. He also became canon of Reims, a post which he held till his death in 1377, honoured and respected as a spiritual leader of his time. He was one of the first of the artist-musicians of the pre-Renaissance period. Even he did not achieve complete freedom in creation; but he worked up his lais, motets, and Masses to the highest pitch of artistry and complexity, showing extraordinary rhythmic subtlety in the use of syncopation, his favourite device, and in his "ballades"—the term includes rondeaux and virelais—he produced a genuine artistic creation, in which at least one subsidiary part was freely invented above a given melody. The "ballade" was an ingeniously constructed song or duet of one or more verses, with one or two supporting or purely ornamental free parts. For well over a century it remained the favourite musical form throughout the Western world. The elaborate artifice of the music had its counterpart in the courtly compliments of the text and the ostentatious splendour of the language, full of learned mythological allusions. Machaut's claim that the ear should be used to check a completed composition was the first indication that the combination of given melodies, the distinguishing characteristic of the old motet style, was beginning to yield to a freer, more individual attitude towards creative art.

In Italy even more than in France the new style of notation was the sign of a spiritual awakening. The music of the early Renaissance, which centred in northern Italy, and Florence in particular, coincided with the first great flights of Italian poetry of the generation after Dante—the work of Boccaccio and Petrarch—and occupied a corresponding posi-

tion in musical history. In place of the stiffness of
tonality characteristic of the "Ars antiqua" there appeared a finer perception of the possibilities of modulation. In place of the old insensitiveness to faults of
part-writing there came a purer style, to which the
theorists gave their support by forbidding parallel
fifths, unisons, and octaves. For the first time there
appeared a free art for the delight of a receptive
public, who appreciated and honoured it as art and
gave it its place in the culture of civilized society.
A surprising abundance of musical forms was suddenly
made evident, and a new conception of artistic unity
drove the motet style into the background. Composers
returned once more with particular pleasure to two-
part writing; but at the same time they began to
contrive new and more individual settings to fit the
stanzas of contemporary poetry, such as the madrigal
and the ballata, and whether the tune was in the
upper or the lower part it was cunningly embellished
with a whole host of *fioriture*. The form was made
still more elaborate and complex by the addition of
preludes, interludes, and postludes for all manner of
instruments. Side by side with this more refined art
song came the resurrection of the old popular "rota"
in an immensely improved form as the "caccia," a
canon for two voices over an original instrumental
bass. The form took the name "caccia" from its text,
which originally presented a hunting-scene or at any
rate some lively incident. Such pieces were the first
examples and the precursors of a long line of vocal
program music.

The removal—at once voluntary and involuntary
—of the papal court from Rome to Avignon was
symbolical of a change in music. Italian art continued at first dependent on the Paris model, and the
south of France bridged the gulf between the more

mature work of the French composers and the vernal music of Italy. But about the middle of the fourteenth century Italy broke free from this dependence —only, it is true, to relapse into it again completely at the end of the century. On both sides of the Apennines, in northern Italy and in Florence, from about 1340 there were active a whole series of minor composers—the earliest names being those of GIOVANNIDA CASCIA and JACOPO DI BOLOGNA—every one of whom had individuality in a greater or lesser degree. At the head of all these comes FRANCESCO LANDINO, the blind organist of San Lorenzo in Florence (d. 1397), master of all instruments of the time, who was crowned king of poets or musicians at Venice in 1364. To see an immediate reflection in literature of the influence of his art, one should read Giovanni da Prato's *Paradiso degli Alberti* or the stories in Boccaccio's *Decamerone*. His likeness has been preserved on his tombstone in San Lorenzo, where he is represented with his little portable organ, still at that time primarily a secular instrument. Poetry and music both reached a new and glorious level of achievement. A large number of the works of the Italian "Ars nova" have come down to us in the so-called Squarcialupi Manuscript in the Laurenziana at Florence, written in the first quarter of the fifteenth century after the fading of this "proto-Renaissance" or forerunner of the Renaissance proper.

With this provision of new forms, added to the old forms of the conductus and the simpler syllabic compositions of polyphonic works, music managed for nearly two hundred years, giving preference now to the one, now to the other, according to the end in view, and learned to handle them, within its limitations, with greater freedom and dexterity. The limitations must not be forgotten. The essence of

the art of the fourteenth and fifteenth centuries lay
in the subordination of accompanying parts, generally for instruments and richly ornamented, to a single principal part (rarely more than one) which was
sung and conformed closely to a song-text, whether
sacred or secular; this principal part was the tenor.
Composers were still confined to the "horizontal"
conception of music, and harmony was the chance
result of the movement of the parts. But it is quite
clear that in this music we are faced with an alliance
of vocal and instrumental elements abundantly rich
in possibilities, however uncertain we may be about
the interpretation of details. The advance of the fifteenth century on the artistic standard of the fourteenth was many-sided and far-reaching. There was
the increase in the number of parts to a normal three
or four. Composers showed an increasing delight in
displaying their melodic creative gifts by the addition of new and different parts to existing compositions. Then what had been free accompanying parts
were themselves placed in the tenor as the basis of
new compositions, and composers delighted to show
their mutual esteem by such borrowings. Moreover
the style of the art song with instrumental accompaniment, as it thrived and blossomed under the care
lavished on it, reacted on the composition of music
for the Church. The hymn, the motet, parts of the
Mass, and ultimately the Mass as a whole were
subjected to a polyphonic treatment in which the
Gregorian melodies were enveloped in a rich instrumental vesture of accompanying parts and added
counterpoints. The need was soon felt to divide up
the Mass by changing the number of voices used in
its several sections, while at the same time it was
considered essential to combine these sections into
an artistic whole through the unity of the tenor or

the uniformity of themes in the upper parts. Both in sacred and secular music of this century we note the increasing habit of developing the subsidiary parts from themes of the principal part, so as to link them together intellectually, to establish aritistic unity not merely by simultaneous combination as in the old motet, but also in the succession of motives. In the rise of a free type of imitation lay the greatest achievement of this century; so great was the enthusiasm with which it cultivated strict canonic writing and made it its boast to move with the highest skill under the greatest restraint.

With regard to the incorporation of the secular style into church music, a distinction must be kept between the forms of the motet (or hymn) and of the separate section of the Mass and the composition of the Mass as a whole. Even in the fifteenth-century motets there were both old and modern types. The old type was still linked up with the early motet of the previous century, which comprised more than one text; it would introduce, for instance, a second text, with allusions to the particular church festival, to be sung at the same time as the liturgical text, the whole being accompanied by one or two additional instrumental or vocal parts. It was this type of motet that the musicians of the time favoured for occasions of very special importance; an example is the work written by ANTONIUS ROMANUS for the enthronement of Doge Tomaso Mocenigo in 1413, a show-piece of the greatest solemnity and magnificence, combining both the ecclesiastical and the secular styles. In the modern type of motet, on the other hand, the dominant role was allotted to one principal part, to which the accompanying parts—usually two lower ones—remained subservient. But with all this subservience there was a

close similarity of character between the parts. It was
as if the old faux-bourdon were coming to life again
in a higher and more artistically conscious sphere of
activity. This does not, however, alter the fact that
fifteenth-century music was a simpler art, less subjective and more popular in character than that of the
fourteenth century.

Isolated sections of the Mass were also treated in
the same way as the motets. The principal source of
the music of this time—the celebrated Trent Manuscripts, which were originally in the cathedral there
and later in Vienna and have been in the possession of
the Italians since 1919, and which contain in all about
1600 works by French, Burgundian, and Flemish
composers—consists principally of such isolated portions of the "Ordo Missæ." Usually the plainsong-
melody lies in the upper part, but it is so obscured by
ornaments, appoggiaturas, and alterations of rhythm,
so individualized and "coloured," that it is by no means
easy to distinguish the essential melody. The "accompaniment" to this part derives from its melodic
inflexions, and there are all sorts of manipulations,
both simple and ingenious, of the subsidiary parts.

Among complete, connected settings of the whole
of the Mass, which are still rare in the middle of
the century, the greater number also have an ornamented liturgical upper part; but all the sections
employ a more or less uniform principal theme, which
serves as an emblem of the relationship between them.
Side by side, however, with this so-called Descant
Mass the Tenor Mass was already beginning to emerge.
The Tenor Mass holds the texture of the parts together from within, as it were, and to this end uses a
liturgical, or more rarely a secular, melody that is
generally free from ornamentation, and repeats this
melody, often with severe rhythmical modifications,

for each section of the Mass. No one troubled very much about whether the tunes had an ecclesiastical flavour. This time of change and unrest, this period of transition from the Middle Ages into modern times, this century at the close of which America was discovered, which was still hesitating between mysticism and humanism, did not distinguish very exactly between ecclesiastical and secular. The appropriation of secular tunes—one of which, *L'Homme armé*, was used by nearly every important musician of the day —went on for over a century and could not be entirely eradicated even by the strict spirit of the Counter-Reformation, which found expression in the resolution of the Council of Trent.

The external history of this development is that of a great artistic achievement, which seems to have started in England at the beginning of the fifteenth century and is associated with the famous name of John Dunstable. His pupil Binchois carried the impulse to the Continent; but Guillaume Dufay, likewise a pupil of Dunstable, bears the greatest name among composers of the time. With him and his followers, Ockeghem, Obrecht, and many others, began the unique pre-eminence of the Netherland School. With Josquin Després's larger personality the movement reached its summit and was carried indeed over the summit into new artistic territory. Singers and composers from the Netherlands, not only in the churches of their fatherland but also in Paris, Burgundy, Rome, and Naples, held the monopoly of artistic composition. In Spain and northern Italy they drove a national art of song, modest but full of promise for the future, completely into the background, though it is true that they occasionally took an active interest in it themselves. Only in Germany was their influence less active; and although for this reason Germany remained a good way behind the advance of the time and did not reach the climax of its mediæval artistic development till the middle of the sixteenth century, German composers were none the less distinguished from the international art of the period by quite definite characteristics of style in organ music (KONRAD PAUMANN) and in hymns and motets (ADAM VON FULDA), by the purity of their melodic style, by the struggle for vital expression and richness of instrumental tone, and by their aversion to the use of mere artifice for its own sake.

One of the theoretical writers of the close of the fifteenth century—indeed, the most important of them all—the Netherlander JOHANNES TINCTORIS (1435 or 1436–1511), who worked at the court of Ferdinand of Aragon in Naples and to whom we owe the first æsthetic and historical judgments and the first little dictionary of musical terms, has recorded the historical fact of the origin of this movement in England. Another proof, still extant, is the so-called Old Hall Manuscript, which contains 138 compositions entirely by English musicians. JOHN DUNSTABLE (c. 1376–1453) was the first to treat a given "cantus firmus" with free ornamentation and to put a free and simple accompaniment to it. A sort of return to the old Celtic pentatonic gave his work a new power and popular appeal. His two pupils Binchois and Dufay carried his art to the Kingdom of Burgundy, which lay between France and Germany and was destroyed before the end of the fifteenth century; this land was of great cultural importance in the formation of social standards, in its conceptions of chivalry and love, and in all the ceremonial of court and city. The Emperor Maximilian I was a later romantic heir of all these ideals. For this aristocratic and middle-class society GILLES BINCHOIS, who was born about 1400 at Bins or

Mons in Hainault, was *maestro di cappella* and chaplain
at the court of Philippe el Bon, and died in 1460 at
Lille, wrote his fifty-odd songs, beside which his
church music is of quite minor importance. They
are astonishingly sensitive and delicate songs—gently
moving voice-parts with two instrumental tenors,
songs of farewell and other love-songs in strophic
form, which had a particularly strong influence on
South German song-writing—an influence which was
still effective at the beginning of the sixteenth century.
GUILLAUME DUFAY was a much more universal type,
one of those composers who represent a whole
century. He was born some time before 1400, probably
at Chimay in Hainault, worked intermittently in the
papal chapel, and died in 1474, a canon at Cambrai.
Dufay's compositions include every type of music of
that time, from chansons and motets of every description to settings of the complete Mass. In the
elegance, polish, sonority, and general character of
his style he embraces all the national elements of his
time. He is French in his chansons, Nordic to a
striking extent in his motets and Masses, Italian in the
grace that informs all that he touches. Like Lassus a
hundred years later, he is one of the great international figures of music.

These three, Dunstable, Binchois, and Dufay, are
commonly grouped together under the title of the
"first Netherland school." If this be accepted, we
must also admit a second Netherland school, in which
a list of important composers is headed by JOHANNES
OCKEGHEM, perhaps the most individual and at any
rate the most imaginative of Dufay's pupils. He was
maestro di cappella and chaplain to Charles VII in
Paris, and died in 1495 at Tours, where he was
treasurer of the Abbey of St. Martin. He is the great
master of the Mass. We have no fewer than seventeen

Masses by him, besides motets and a few chansons. He must be regarded as the chief exponent of the peculiar craftsmanship of the Netherland school, which consisted in a preference for canonic writing and the taste for developing from a single melody a polyphonic movement according to prescribed rules (often expressed in the form of a riddle) by placing several different time-signatures at the beginning—a taste that would seem to prefer ingenuity of construction to vital expression or a wealth of melodic invention. Undoubtedly, too, mystical signs and purposes play a part in this sort of craftsmanship; music becomes an edifice of sound, as for example in Ockeghem's *Deo gratias* for thirty-six voices, which is in canon throughout. With JACOB OBRECHT (b. at Utrecht in 1430, d. at Ferrara in 1505), the most important composer of the third Netherland school, who worked at Cambrai, Bruges, and Antwerp and in Italy, this art of construction grew less complex under Southern influence. Obrecht began as an exponent of "linear counterpoint," but gradually changed to a style of writing in which the texture was clearer and the harmonic basis well defined. His large output numbers twenty-four Masses, twenty-two motets, a *St. Matthew Passion* for several voices, and a quantity of secular works; his influence was enormous.

JOSQUIN DESPRÉS was probably born in Hainault about 1450. He is known to have been a singer in the chapel at the court of the Sforzas at Milan, in the Vatican chapel at Rome, and at Cambrai, Modena, possibly Paris, and Ferrara. He died in 1521, a prebendary of Condé. Like Claudio Monteverdi in the seventeenth century, he summed up all the achievements of the fifteenth century and, filling them with new meaning, transmitted them to the sixteenth. His work—thirty Masses, many motets and chansons—re-

mained the model for his generation and that which
followed it; and so great was his importance that
no musician of his day could remain unaffected by it.
He increased the number of parts to six and employed
all the constructive skill and craftsmanship of the
fifteenth century, not so much for its own sake as to
impart an entirely individual expression to it. Not
that his music is an illustration of the text; but he
seizes the spirit of his subject—earnest, tender, solemn,
or majestic—with a passionate precision. In him was
attained the ideal of "Gothic" church music—universal in style and yet a personal creation. And if we
take into account his contemporaries as well—the
pensive and gentle PIERRE DE LA RUE, the genial AN-
TOINE BRUMEL, the brilliant LOYSET COMPÈRE, and
many others—the high water-mark of genuine church
music would seem to be, not in Palestrina's day, but
already at this time, on the threshold of the Renaissance.

Of the German composers who from the modest
beginnings of an indigenous polyphonic style of song-
compositions—the principal source of this music being
the *Locheimer Liederbuch*, compiled after the middle
of the century—came to throw in their lot with the
"international" music of the Netherland school, only
two need be mentioned: HEINRICH ISAAK and ALEX-
ANDER AGRICOLA. Isaak was actually of Flemish origin,
and through his activity in Italy—at Ferrara and
Florence—and his extensive travels was one of the
most "international" composers of the time. But he was
a German none the less; and that not merely on account of his service at the court of Archduke Sigismund at Innsbruck and in the many households of
the Emperor Maximilian—at Augsburg, Vienna, and
Constance—but also by reason of his natural incli-
nations. He died in 1517 at Florence. He is at home

in all styles—in Italian songs, chansons, Masses, and in his great cycle of motets, the *Choralis Constantinus*, written for the cathedral at Constance. But he is most himself in German song. His song of farewell, *Innsbruck ich muss dich lassen*, with its individual melody in the upper part, was in spite of its modest scope, an epoch-making piece of music, just as Mozart's *Veilchen* was two hundred and fifty years later. Alexander Agricola also travelled much. He was *maestro di cappella* at Milan, Cambrai, Mantua (with the Gonzagas), and finally at the court of Philippe le Beau in Burgundy, in whose service he died at Valladolid, probably in 1506. He, too, exerted an international influence with his Masses, chansons, and Italian songs.

This international influence was made possible by the invention of music-printing about 1500. This produced as great a revolution in the history of music as book-printing had done in the history of general European culture. A quarter of a century after Gutenberg's first attempts, German and Italian printers produced printed missals. The decisive step—the printing of the notation of measured music from type—was taken by Ottaviano dei Petrucci of Fossombrone, who worked at Venice and in his native town. His editions of Masses, motets, chansons, and "frottole" put all later examples out of the running by their perfection. Venice, following his example, remained the principal centre for the printing and publishing of polyphonic music. But this "black art" also spread throughout Europe with amazing rapidity, and nowhere more so than in Germany and France.

THE "RENAISSANCE"

New Forms

IT IS tempting to maintain that the sixteenth century was more than any other period in the development of music a time of transition—a time spent in putting the finishing touches to what had already been done and in preparing the ground for what was yet to come. We find two streams flowing side by side, one ebbing, the other rising; between them there are connexions, both seen and unseen, which give the music of this century its peculiar brilliance and dazzling contrasts. The taste of the last years of the Middle Ages was all in favour of strict imitations, the cultivation of the canon in the simplest and most recondite forms of inversion, diminution, and augmentation. The mediæval ideal of music based on construction was magnificently realized in the sixteenth century, particularly in the composition of Masses and motets. It is true that certain technical tricks of the preceding period, such as the development of a polyphonic work from a single part, were abandoned. But in strictness of composition and genuine craftsmanship there are a large number of Masses and motets of the sixteenth century that are in no way inferior to the technical achievements of men like Ockeghem and Obrecht. Indeed, this art of ingenious and skilful combination enjoyed an astonishing new lease of life at the end of this century and the beginning of the next.

But at the same time a completely new spirit pervades the music of the sixteenth century. The chief sign of this is a change in the relationship between the vocal and instrumental elements in a musical composition, between the chief melody and the accompanying parts. The period up to about 1520 may be characterized as that of rich and varied cultivation of song accompanied by voices or instruments. But from now on, the general structure of vocal composition was controlled by instrumental principles, though the individual constituents were motifs following vocal laws and inspired by poetic fancies. In this way the shape of the new motet and madrigal originated. These forms show that a totally new conception of the unity of a work of art had once more been arrived at, a new sense of relationship between superior and subordinate elements. The old unity of calculated construction was succeeded by a new poetic unity, resulting from the free play of the artist's imagination. A work no longer depended on

a given melody running through it to hold it together;
the composer shaped and unified it, as it were, with
his own hands. For the first time he employed
contrast freely, as his text demanded, between homophony and imitation and between few and many
voice-parts. Especially in the working of motifs in free
imitation he now gained a wonderfully delicate instrument of expression. The music of the fifteenth century
had been full of ingenuity and intellectual contriv-
ance; what the sixteenth century contributed was
the directly sensuous, poetic expression of an idea.
We find these two attitudes most wonderfully reconciled in Bach, who may be said in this sense to have
succeeded to an artistic inheritance that was centuries
old.

Throughout the century the motet forms the en-
thralling scene of conflict between the old and new
tendencies. There were several subdivisions of the
form, treated in a more or less conservative or progressive style—the psalm-settings fall into the latter
category—and of its composers some inclined to old,
others to new methods, one of the most impetuous
being Orlandus Lassus. But the true outlet for the
advanced movement, the arena for all innovation and
experiment, was the madrigal, in which all the possibilities of expression of that age were first combined.
Originating from the fifteenth-century frottole—small
strophic songs, half-serious in character, still for the
most part instrumentally accompanied—its musical
pattern at first clearly imitated the form of the sonnet
and the canzona. But it did so with purely vocal
means, chiefly, to begin with, in four-part, preferably
homophonic songs. At the same time it fundamentally
changed its tone; it sought nobility and fastidious
refinement to the point of extravagance and sentimental affectation. With ADRIAN WILLAERT, however,

and especially with his pupil CIPRIANO DE RORE there began a fuller development of its resources. Five voices became the norm, and with this the choral web grew subtler and richer in colour. Homophonic and imitatively handled sections alternated; the chorus was cunningly subdivided to throw individual lines of the poem into relief. Tonality came to be treated more freely and boldly. Rore initiated a chromaticism which later, especially in the compositions of LUCA MARENZIO and GESUALDO DA VENOSA, was to lead to extremes of daring—but not based upon clear harmonic perception and hence not fully absorbed by the main stream of development.

Above all, however, the madrigal brought about a new conception of the motif as a symbol. The composer sought an expression that would exactly match the poem of his choice. The motif was no longer to be a mere garment, so to speak, for the text; it was to be as precisely expressive as the text itself. The laborious efforts of madrigalists in this direction often betrayed them into a naïve tone-painting in which they lost sight of the work as a whole in the detail; but the close observation of nature involved was a step towards true poetic expression. Towards the end of the sixteenth century the madrigal became more and more infused with dramatic life, and this despite the number of its voice-parts and a seemingly inappropriate form. In the numerous dialogues the tendency shows itself conspicuously. Anyone acquainted with the admirable character-studies contained in MONTEVERDI's madrigals, for instance, will realize from them alone that here we are standing on the threshold of modern art. The madrigal is a wonderful product of vital emancipated music, worthy of the Renaissance. Its clear-cut, individualized structure bears witness to the finest social culture. The diversity, the refinement of its expression, the exhaustive development of its resources by its best exponents are unsurpassed and unsurpassable.

So far, that is to say, as the resources of the medium went; but the limitations of that pure a-cappella art render it essentially different in expression from music of later times. Wherein does its strangeness lie? Not so much in the tonality of the madrigalists—for in the trend during the century towards the major and minor modes those progressions of unrelated chords so charming to our ears occurred less and less frequently—as in a wealth of rhythmical effects, the result of their peculiar conception of independent part-writing. And then in their different attitude towards construction and dynamic effects. The age of a-cappella music was certainly not ignorant of accumulative and intensifying devices—at any rate, after part-writing for more than four voices came in, and especially when use was made of multiple choirs—but the art was not yet learned of intensifying by means of the organization of contrasting sections, of that inner musical intensification attained by the dramatically conceived development of a theme or themes. In the language of exaggeration one might say that an a-cappella piece, provided it reached a satisfying length and preserved unity of tonality, could come to an end where it chose. It was this placidity of movement, this perpetual ebb and flow, this seemingly inexhaustible outpouring of melody, that so captivated the Catholic enthusiasts of the romantic movement in the nineteenth century. But towards the close of the sixteenth century came the time for contrasting themes to appear in the madrigal, and with them the first attempts at structure and cumulative effects in the modern sense.

In the course of the century the leadership of the

world of music passed to Italy, and the process is clearly to be followed in the history of the madrigal. In the fifteenth century, at the time when she was making her way to cultural predominance, Italy had played a subordinate role in musical art. It is significant that Lorenzo de' Medici, when he wished to hear one of his canzones artistically set to music, had to apply through his organist Antonio Squarcialupi to a Northerner, Guillaume Dufay. In the first half of the sixteenth century the Netherlands still dominated musical Italy. But as time went on, the Italians so assimilated the achievements of the foreigner that by the end of the century they represented, with the forms they had cultivated (madrigal, villanella, canzonetta, balletto) and their vocal (double chorus) and instrumental style (ricercar, canzon francese, toccata), the foremost artistic power of the age and set the standard for Germany, England, and, to a lesser degree, France. The later Netherlanders no longer set the fashion for Italy; they themselves were already under the siren's spell, which few could resist.

Not that Italy reached this position single-handed. The brilliant artistic attainments of the century were only possible, and are only comprehensible, through the competition of the various musical nations. There was an incessant give-and-take, a perpetual appropriating and remodelling. The international character of art, the interest in foreign achievements and their ungrudging and swift assimilation—something that later only German music was to carry on, to its prosperity and peril—never flourished so easily and surely as at that time. The principal contribution made by the French was in the form of the chanson—a contribution, light in content while enormous in bulk, of an airy, sprightly music, full of pretty babblings and devoted to sentimental love-ditties, with a preference

for a tone of refined *grivoiserie*. A peculiarity of
this literature, which soon came to be imitated
everywhere, was programmatic description by purely
vocal means, in the manner of the old Florentine
caccia—of street noises, battle scenes, and the war-
bling of birds—in most cases applied to an ono-
matopœic text. Through the simplicity and clarity
of its form and themes the chanson, transformed into
the canzon francese, greatly influenced the budding
instrumental music. While the ricercar was the ancestor of the fugue, the chanson was the soil out of
which the sonata was to grow. The modern variation
form seems to have had its original home in Spain.
A development similiar in many respects to that of
Italy and contemporary with it took place there,
political ties connecting that country equally with
Italy and the Netherlands. Spain produced a large
number of church composers of the highest rank,
peculiarly distinguished by the glowing mysticism of
their expression. Here at an early date the variation
form seems to have originated, based upon a recognition of the harmonic foundations of the theme. We
possess lute variations by Spanish masters of the 1530's,
variations for viola da gamba of the year 1553, and
keyboard variations of the same period, especially by
the great master Antonio de Cabezon, which do not
differ in principle from the achievements of Bach,
Beethoven, and Brahms.

Such was the field of art which the teeming composers of the Netherlands, France, England, Germany, Spain, and Italy made amazingly productive.
Among them were figures of the most pronounced
individuality. The representatives of the period,
GIOVANNI PIERLUIGI DA PALESTRINA and ORLANDUS
LASSUS, count among the great men of Western

civilization—Palestrina as the composer of the ideal
type of church music, pure, purged of all subjectivity, marvellously harmonious, Lassus as the most
versatile and vigorously creative master of the
motet, madrigal, villanella, and chanson. These two absorbed and fulfilled the entire musical art of their age.
Palestrina (1525–94), who from 1571 was *maestro di
cappella* at St. Peter's in Rome, was heir to all the
traditions of his Roman predecessors and was also
steeped in the music of the Netherlanders, which he
transfused into an expression of utter purity and
immaculate, unearthly longing. Lassus (1532–94), a
Fleming, from 1556 head of the Munich court chapel,
found decisive stimulus for his art in the Italian
madrigal. Palestrina was master of the Mass—we
possess ninety-three four- to eight-part Masses by
him—Lassus of the motet (the huge collection of his
motets, *Magnum Opus Musicum*, contains over five
hundred examples), as also of the madrigal, villanella,
chanson, and German Lied, all of which he mastered
like his mother-tongue. The two were as equally great
in creative power as they were different in nature.
The one commanded a serene flow of music, raising
it to supernal heights; the other was full of explosive
strength, of dramatic vitality controlled with effort.
The one was a lover of songful melisma; the other
of vigorous declamation. The one was essentially a
church composer (his secular madrigals are of hardly
any importance either in his life-work or in the
history of the genre); the other in his madrigals the
noble singer of love both sensual and supersensual, in
his chansons of sportive *joie de vivre*, and in his villa-
nellas a forerunner of the commedia dell' arte. A veritable Proteus was Lassus, with his power of changing
his musical style; indeed, one of the greatest masters of

all time in his virile strength, his unconquerable creative urge, his force of expression, his keen sense of the comic.

While Rome, through Palestrina and his pupils, became more than ever the focus of musical life in Italy, the influence of the powerful Venetian school, through ANDREA and GIOVANNI GABRIELI, uncle and nephew, reached out beyond the frontiers of Italy. Palestrina and Lassus inherited and perfected an art which was nearing its maturity; but with Giovanni Gabrieli music seems to have burst into fresh bloom. At Venice a style of composition for several choirs prevailed, founded by Willaert and cultivated by his successors Rore, Zarlino, Andrea Gabrieli, Donato, and Croce. Instead of single voices, a work was built upon the question and answer, the timbre, the echo, the tonal combination of differently constituted choirs of voices and instruments. Giovanni Gabrieli brought this style to the zenith of its effect. He did more: through a new disposition of vocal and instrumental elements and the invention of a new kind of motif, he led the way into untrodden territory. A personality at once conservative and daring, preserving and augmenting, he avoided the mistake that contemporary and later choral composers committed, of relying on the merely passing effect. His music was brilliant, yet profound; festive, yet for the Church—albeit a specifically Venetian Church; full of power, romance, and wonderfully glowing colour. His *Symphoniæ Sacræ* (1597 and 1615) was the decisive work of a new trend in choral composition.

With the Gabrielis not only was the way paved for a relation between choir and orchestra that was to remain permanently valid; but also the separation of vocal and instrumental music-making was completed. We have noticed already how purely instru-

mental laws governed the structure of the new musical
product of the sixteenth century. Through the trans-
ference of vocal pieces to instruments—to the organ
and to ensembles of strings and wood-wind—inher-
ently instrumental forms gradually came to detach
themselves from the hitherto undifferentiated pattern.
Out of the motet, with its various subdivisions, came
the ricercar (a fugue with several themes in succession) and the fantasia (a fugue with a single theme),
the latter eventually supplanting the ricercar, which
was the form more cultivated in the sixteenth century.
Out of the chanson the canzon francese, the prototype
of the sonata, developed. The most valuable elements
that the canzon adopted from its vocal model were
the rhythmic precision and animation of its motifs
and the lucid harmonic lay-out of its form. Con-
current with this was the development of the instrumental dance, which cultivated a wealth of forms,
ceasing more and more to be mere *Gebrauchsmusik*,
supplying themes for variations and already at this
early period assembling a cycle of dance forms to
create the suite. Along with the development of form
went the improvement of performance; the pursuit
of instrumental style was accompanied by the evolution of the particular technics of the domestic keyboard instruments, of the organ, and of string and
wood-wind instruments. The virtuoso appeared, at
first on the lute, the favourite instrument of the time.
German organ-playing of this time, with its conventional "colourists," had nothing to compare with the
Italians' handling of the strict and free forms of
ricercar, prelude, and toccata—the solo piece *par
excellence*—and still less with the English, whose music
for the virginal, in which they especially cultivated
variations and the toccata, was a genuine, astonishingly subtle keyboard art. Towards the end of the

century the canzon francese divides (though not
always very sharply) into two separate types—the
Sonata for wind instruments and the Canzona for
strings. The former is a fully scored piece of festal
music, the latter chamber music, more lightly scored
and more delicately wrought. The one is the ancestor of the symphony and the concerto, the other of
the chamber sonata. An important part was played
in the whole instrumental art of the sixteenth century by the practice of improvising ornamentation.

For a century and more the Venetian school, with
Andrea and Giovanni Gabrieli at its head, exercised
a decisive influence on Germany and the Netherlands
by their instruction in every branch of music. Andrea
Gabrieli was the teacher of HANS LEO HASLER and,
with Zarlino, of JAN PETERSZOON SWEELINCK (1562–
1621), who in turn was to hand on the tradition to a
whole succession of considerable German musicians.
Giovanni Gabrieli's teaching speaks for itself in the
fact that HEINRICH SCHÜTZ was his pupil. But even
had he not had many other pupils, the favourable
position of Venice and the magic of his music still
have induced German music to follow in the wake
of the Bucintoro.

As in a remote little flower-garden, Germany had
until then cultivated her secular song. For long the
technique of the form, deriving from the fifteenth
century and having little in common with the free
methods of the later age, had remained the same.
Following the style of the court song, the words
and tunes of which were kept in circulation by
wandering minstrels, this German secular song presents a more or less artful interweaving of parts,
generally capable of either vocal or instrumental ex-
ecution, twining around the melody sung by the tenor.
After the three-part writing of the *Locheimer Lie-*

derbuch these songs were normally composed, at the hey-day of their vogue about 1530, in four or, at the most, five parts. A simple form, closely matching that of the verse, was preferred to the pretentious architecture of the motet. Two-part counterpoint occurs characteristically, with graceful cadences, a preference for the Lydian mode, and withal a refined and charming rhythmic pattern calculated to enhance the air. Chiefly they were, of course, love-songs; but some were occupational songs, and sentiments of an edifying, reflective, and also political nature found utterance. A special place was taken by drinking-songs and convivial ditties, the expression of a robust material enjoyment, culminating in the quodlibet, with its innumerable quips and allusions. The scope of this lyricism, ranging from homely heartiness and tenderness to simple grandeur, shows how wide must have been the response it could count upon from the German people and how deep-rooted it was in their hearts. An indication of this is the fact that no composer ever published a collection consisting entirely of his own songs. In contrast to the exclusive and subjective art of the madrigal, these songs represented a sheer gift to the community. They are preserved in a few large anthologies, the most important of which, containing 380 songs, is the five-volume collection (1539–56) of the art-loving physician Georg Forster. Among a large number of more or less unimportant craftsmen the outstanding composers after HEINRICH ISAAK—who, true German that he was, hit the nail straight on the head—were HEINRICH FINCK, THOMAS STOLTZER (d. 1526), PAUL HOFHAIMER, organist to the Emperor Maximilian, and, above all, ARNOLD VON BRUCK and the Swiss LUDWIG SENFL. The last of these especially was a writer of masterly songs, tender or noble or, again, full of humour. He ranged over the whole gamut of song from the rude and racy to the sublime. The homophonic settings of verses in classical metres by Hofhaimer and Senfl have a curious place of their own beside these songs. The humanistic movement which in Italy urged men to a vigorous creative renewal of the spirit of antiquity took on in Germany the character of pedantry. In the last thirty years of the century the ground where those blossoms had flowered seemed to dry up. Italian influence and actual importations of Italian music had an easy conquest. A number of artists, indeed, attempted to introduce certain ingredients from the South into the homemade brew, now running so thin; but the attempt failed.

Things were different in England. In the past she had given a new impulse to the whole of European music, and she still retained her rightful position beside the other nations. She produced such fine ecclesiastical composers as CHRISTOPHER TYE and ROBERT WHITE and set beside the grand and noble simplicity of the church music of THOMAS TALLIS (d. 1585) the more personal, more subjective, more imaginative art of WILLIAM BYRD (d. 1623), one of the most distinguished composers of the age. In 1588 the Italian madrigal and canzonetta in their maturity crossed the Alps and came to England, where they continued to flourish in English dress for, roughly, thirty years. Composers like MORLEY, WILBYE, and WEELKES gave the madrigal an extraordinary increase of intensity and the canzonetta an added grace. Their music was worthy of the age for which Shakspere wrote. Between 1588 and 1627 more than forty books of madrigals appeared, ranging from Byrd's *Psalms, Sonnets and Songs for five voices* to Hilton's *Airs or Fa-las for three voices*. Among them was Morley's collection *The Triumphs of Oriana* (1601), the title and arrangement of which were a close imitation of the Itailan *Trionfo di Dori* (1592). The Italian collection having been dedicated to a Venetian lady, *The Triumphs of Oriana* was published as an act of homage to Queen Elizabeth; it included contributions from twenty-three composers. This close relationship to all the various forms of the later Italian madrigal, from two-part songs to setting for double choir, remained unchanged throughout the work of Byrd, Morley, Weelkes, Wilbye, Farmer, Farnaby, East, Bateson, Lichfield, Pilkington, Tomkins, and Gibbons; and this is equally true of the lyrical madrigal, with its wealth of subjective expression, of the saucy canzonetta, and of the gay and cheerful ballet. Many of the texts were translations of Italian models, but a large number also were characteristic and original poems.

It would be a mistake to regard the English madrigal as a mere imitation of its Italian forebear. These English composers did not make "originality" their specific aim, and they were quite ingenuous in the way in which they took over the forms of Gabrieli, Marenzio, and Vecchi. But their music is shot through and through with the spirit of a more abundant, more essential, more virile feeling for melody. Instead of the Italian conventionality and over-refinement of expression we find a more personal spirit, a more robust and more natural emotion, not to mention a greater certainty, instinctively acquired, in the handling of harmony and rhythm. The individuality of all these composers is clearly marked: William Byrd, the greatest artist of them all, for all his severe restraint; Thomas Morley, his pupil, particularly devoted to the light and graceful ballet; Thomas Weelkes, subjective and unequal in achievement; above all, John Wilbye, an inspired composer and master of all the resources of expression, who shows not only the greatest daring

but also the most finished taste. The composers of the
later generation, such as ORLANDO GIBBONS, JOHN
WARD, and THOMAS TOMKINS, used themes and thematic contrasts that already foreshadowed, as in the
works of the contemporary Italians, the end of music
of this type. At the same time the English madrigal
—thanks to the devotion to tradition shown by a few
music-lovers—was kept alive for over three centuries,
and a direct connexion can be traced between it and
the vocal music of England at the present day.

Germany, on the other hand, soon gave up the
struggle and preferred to write purely Italian madrigals. The Italian villanella also appeared, first in its
own tongue, though it took on a superficially German character when it became a "Bauerliedlein"—
superficially, since in Italy the three-part villanella
was almost entirely dedicated to parody and could
be fully appreciated only within the convention of,
and as a contrast to, an exceedingly sophisticated
state of culture. A very curious turn was taken
when these songs were adapted to suit "Christian,
edifying and moral" sentiments. Later, through the
example of Gastoldi and Vecchi, the canzona for
several voices (generally five) and the balletto started
their triumphant progress through Germany, where
they were to enjoy a career far more lasting and
influential than in the country of their origin. The
balletto found its way into the dance-suite and also
brought fresh vigour—again through the example of
Vecchi and Banchieri—to the old quodlibet, giving rise
to a whole literature of choruses and songs of a folk-
character, which, above all in central and southern
Germany, succeeded in maintaining its place in the
domestic music of the country with refreshing vitality
and came to light again at the beginning of the
eighteenth century.

The foreign plant was first really acclimatized by
HANS LEO HASLER of Nuremberg. Not that he was
the first to draw from the wells of Italian art; but the
way in which he absorbed that spirit and then brought
it forth to new life—the way, for instance, in which
in his *Neue deutsche Liedlein* (1591) he transformed
the Italian canzonetta from a parodistic or pseudo-
pastoral form into a choral song instinct with more
sincere feeling and charm—is a most significant illustration of the relationship of German music to foreign
influences. From this point of view Hasler was actually
the true forerunner—in contrast to the numerous
composers like Hasse and Graun—of Schütz, Handel,
and Mozart.

Among Hasler's works special importance attaches
to the *Psalmen und christliche Gesänge* (1607) and the
Kirchengesänge: Psalmen und geistliche Lieder (1608).
They bear witness to the measure in which this Italianate musician was attached to that simple yet so
significant expression of the spirit of the German
Reformation, the communal song of the Protestant
Church—the chorale. In those stern times the chorale
had come to include practically the whole of German
song, secular as much as religious, and within the
narrowest frame work had become crystallized into a
form as capable of the profoundest symbolism as it was
of surviving the wear and tear of generations. In
1523 and 1526 Luther had provided the evangelical
service with a new liturgical form which, after having
at first been in the hands of the clergy and choir, made
room, even in the time of the great reformer himself, for increasing participation by the congregation.
Instead of their allotted portions of the Mass, of
matins and of vespers, the members of the congregation now sang hymns before and after the sermon
and at the end of the service—hymns derived from

all manner of sources. Some originated from Gregorian
chants, others from pre-Reformation sacred folk-songs,
while new sources of secular folk-songs were always
being drawn upon. Among the most notable appro-
priations from the secular domain were the psalm-
tunes in use in the Calvinistic Church, arranged in
four-part harmony by CLAUDE GOUDIMEL from French
chanson-melodies and introduced to German con-
gregations in a translation by Ambrosius Lobwasser,
a professor at Königsberg (1573).

This priceless treasure of melody was to have an
eventful history. In the *Geystliche Gesangkbüch-
leyn* of JOHANN WALTHER (1524), Luther's musical
adviser, and again in *Newe deudsche geistliche Ge-
senge* by GEORG RHAW (1544) and in other less
important works, these melodies are artistically arranged with a view both to domestic devotions and
to performance by the trained church choir, with the
tune in the tenor according to the contemporary
German usage. By the end of the century, however,
the tune had made its way into the treble. The artist
with his personal feelings had effaced himself behind
the symbolic act of congregational prayer. Such a
treatment of the chorale as is found in Hasler's *Psalms*
(the production of 1607 mentioned above) where the
chorale is "*fugweis componiert*" (fugally treated)
became the exception. The general rule was to leave
the chorale untouched—"*simpliciter gesetzt.*" It is only
necessary to recall the highest development of this
art—J. S. Bach's chorales—to realize how wide a
scope for poetic interpretation was afforded to composers in the harmony and part-writing of this kind
of arrangement. The symbolic content of the chorale
found its supreme expression in pure instrumental
music, in compositions for the organ. Of decisive
importance here was the *Tabulatura nova* of the Halle

organist SAMUEL SCHEIDT (1624), whose chorale arrangements lead straight to the art of the great Protestant organ school and to the Bach cantana.

Accompanied Monody

Viewed as a whole, the sixteenth century was one of the most extraordinary periods of conflict in the history of music. It is true that, in spite of the open warfare between old and new, in which rival pens played their part, it passed more quietly than similar contentions in later times—those, for example, that raged round Gluck and about the "New German" school. But the conflict was there none the less. From the beginning of the century every composer had to find his own answer to questions that affected his very essence as an artist; he had to resolve in himself the struggle between homophony and polyphony, between the differing claims of vocal and instrumental expression, between melody as the servant of language and as the vehicle for ornament. Only the greatest masters, the composers of all-embracing genius, found it easy to reconcile the conflicting claims and instinctively hit upon the right solution in every branch of music. National divisions were revealed by the different tendencies. The Germans and Netherlanders pursued an ideal of instrumental polyphony, rich in harmonic possibilities—the organ chorale and the fugue—which also had a decisive influence on their vocal writing. The Italians, on the other hand, aimed at perfecting instrumental melody, an ideal that pointed the way to the sonata, the concerto, and the aria. In Haydn's sonata form these various currents were one day to be harmonized and reconciled.

One of the practical evidences of this period of conflict and its actual outcome was music-drama or opera, which appeared in its first rough outlines in the last decade of the sixteenth century. Opera involves the co-operation of several arts and many factors. Its origins, therefore, are many and deeply rooted in the past, and the separate ingredients that conditioned the particular form of the new art are clearly distinguished. This form was determined in the first place by the Italian intermezzo. It was customary in the dramatic performances that took place before the aristocratic audiences of the Italian courts to fill up the entr'actes with dances and scenic representations, generally taken from classical mythology, the aim being to excite wonder and astonishment by a novel and decorative spectacle. Soon, however, there was a change of method. Scenes of this kind began to be enlivened by action and eventually they were combined together into a dramatic whole in much the same way as later, in the eighteenth century, opera buffa developed out of the comic intermezzo. An impetus was given to this development by the allegorical festival-play produced to celebrate some event at court, in which words were indispensable. From another starting-point the masquerade tended in the same direction. Its original form, which for long remained the same, was the carnival song—those licentious stanzas which a small troupe of mummers directed at the ladies who were present at the festival. In the second half of the century the tone of these songs became more refined and there was more variety in the invention. The carnival song began to be treated dramatically and its character became more like that of the intermezzo. Finally, in the course of the century music was used more and more in the choruses and dances of the pastoral drama. This had evolved from dramatic eclogues modelled on those of Theocritus and Virgil. As time went on, its popularity increased so much that it became the delight of the whole age. After Tasso's *Aminta* the masterpiece in this form was Guarini's *Pastor fido,* which was idolized by the fashionable world. It was in the realm of classical mythology and pastoral drama that opera was launched on its career.

In this hybrid dramatic form there had begun to appear quite early, in addition to choruses and dances, solo songs accompanied by a single instrument—lute, lyre, or bass viol—or by more imposing instrumental forces. No one can follow the history of these festival performances in the various capitals—first at Venice and then particularly at Ferrara under the auspices of the Este family and at Florence under the Medici—without noticing how such solo songs borrowed from the forms of vocal music current at the time—the frottola, the canzonetta, and, above all, the madrigal in all its stages of development. Experiments of this kind brought nearer a problem whose solution was to be one of the greatest achievements of the Renaissance—the problem of genuine monody—that is, melody sung by a single voice with instrumental accompaniment. Composers were at first content to take a madrigal in several parts, which would naturally be polyphonic in conception, and extract a single part, generally the top one, turning it into a vocal solo and fitting the other voices underneath it as instrumental accompanying parts. This solo voice-part was lavishly ornamented by means of coloratura. The weakness of this experiment from the point of

view of style was, however, soon realized. It was seen
that the isolation of a single part above the others
was arbitrary and artificial, and the vocal embellishment of the solo was superficial and inimical to
true expression. In the composition of songs there
was a movement towards preserving the distinctness of
the poet's words, and in the drama towards a faithful
interpretation of emotion.

There was in Florence a dilettante circle, composed of amateurs, poets and musicians who were
inspired by idealistic conceptions of the might and
majesty of classical drama. Here the new movement
found a formulation of its theoretical principles and
an attempt at their practical realization. The demand
that the text should be intelligible was not new. The
Church had more than once condemned the impro-
priety of the simultaneous use of different texts in
motets and Masses. We know, too, what importance
the Council of Trent assigned not only to the purely
moral but also to the æsthetic question. The delegates
were anxious that the service of God should not be
profaned by the introduction of secular songs; but
they were equally insistent that sacred words should
have their proper value in polyphonic settings.

The members of the Florentine circle went farther, rejecting polyphony as detrimental to poetry.
The struggle against counterpoint, however, was only
the negative part of their program. Of their positive
endeavour—to achieve true accompanied solo song
—the first examples, by VINCENZO GALILEI, have not
survived; but we have a number of later attempts,
first among them some small-scale lyrical settings by
the Roman composer GIULIO CACCINI, published in
1602 under the proud title *Nuove Musiche*. They
consist of madrigals and strophic songs composed
with a meticulous regard for metrical accuracy. They

are not without a certain melodic charm, and the composer, who was himself a singer, was not afraid to introduce vocal ornamentation, although the program of the new school expressly excluded coloratura. The voice-part is supported by a bass of the simplest type, the realization of the harmony being left for the accompanist to improvise. These miniatures were followed in 1597 by JACOPO PERI's *Dafne*, the first drama to be set to music throughout. With the production at Florence in 1600 of two settings of *Euridice* by Caccini and Peri and of Emilio Cavalieri's *Rappresentazione di anima e di corpo*, opera and sacred music-drama made their first public appearance.

The origin of opera in æsthetic principles was a complete contradiction of all the conditions that should attend the birth of a genuine creative work of art; but the Florentine movement nevertheless gave a strong impulse to its growth. This was particularly so in the case of the recitative, with which their arguments were principally concerned. It combined originally the elements of both the declamatory and the lyrical styles; but gradually a separation of the two took place, and the result was the emergence of pure declamation and pure melody—the aria. The other ingredient of the new monody, the basso continuo, seems to have been an assimilation and adaptation of a practice which polyphony had already made its own towards the end of the sixteenth century in another form—the "basso seguente." When works for several voices or several choirs—particularly those of the Venetian and northern Italian school—were performed, it often happened that there was a lack of sufficient vocal and instrumental resources. The organist then had to help things out by accompanying the whole work in unison with the voices. But this meant that he had to have a complete organ score in

tablature before him, the writing of which involved
the expenditure of much time and trouble and, considering the enormous amount of music used, was
practically out of the question. The necessity for
something simpler and the increased understanding
of harmony led to the adoption of an abbreviated
notation—the mere indication of a continuous bass
line, going with whatever happened at any moment
to be the lowest part, on which the expert reader built
up the whole harmonic superstructure of the work.
A simple system of figures written under or above
the notes showed the deviations from the root positions of common chords—that is, chords of the
sixth and six-four, suspensions, and discords. The
adoption of this system, which remained in force for
over a hundred and fifty years, was made easier by
the choral style of the Venetian school, which was
generally homophonic in character. It was the *maestro
di cappella* at St. Mark's, Venice, GIOSEFFO ZARLINO,
who laid the foundations of modern conceptions of
harmony in his *Istituzioni armoniche* and so created a
system on which the whole art of continuo-playing
depended. In this art the feeling for harmony continued throughout the seventeenth century until it
culminated in Bach's miraculous instinct. It has generally been associated with the name of the northern
Italian composer LODOVICO GROSSI DA VIADANA, but it
was actually much older; it came into existence quite
quietly and unobtrusively, and Viadana only put into
writing in a clear if still rather primitive manner the
rules for accompanying and emphasized the necessity
for accepting a limited number of parts as a postulate.
In his hundred *Concerti ecclesiastici* for one, two,
three, and four voices (1602 and 1608) he supplied
a kind of practical manifesto which had an important
influence.

The basso continuo radically changed the whole form and shape of musical composition down to its smallest constituents. Along with music in several parts, there was now music in a few parts, in which the voices were brought together in an entirely new relationship, while the bass absorbed, so to speak, what had previously been the middle parts and became in a way an antithesis to the melodic line of the song or the upper parts. By accepting a subordinate and supporting role it set the upper parts free and allowed them to appear in a new guise— as concerted music. Meanwhile the whole social organization of music had changed. Music made its way from the middle-class parlour to the gilded halls of the aristocracy. In the past there had been a general desire to make music, to take part in a concerted whole. From now onwards the virtuoso was to come to the fore and display his gifts. For reasons both of circumstance and of the nature of the art itself the chief embodiment of the new ideals was found among the composers of the Latin countries.

The form that the bass itself was to take now became a problem. In strictly monodic works it was originally completely subservient to the voice-part, which took its expression from the text; it was a mere harmonic foundation in long sustained notes. It remained so, in fact, in secco recitative as long as that tradition lasted. But more conservative composers— those of the Roman school, for example—treated the bass vocally and so preserved the original melodic character of the continuo. One of the best and simplest ways in which the contemporary feeling for form could be satisfied consisted in the repetition in the bass of a set theme—either long or short—over which the upper parts could develop freely without, however, sacrificing their dependence on the foun-

dation. This device was known as the basso ostinato.
Its use provided a reinforcement to music in the new
concerted style and enabled it to form a properly
balanced whole. By the end of the seventeenth century composers had succeeded in the invention of free
basses which bore an artistically complete relation to
the melodic concerted parts. Once again the bass gradually became a member with equal rights in a polyphonic body; and once it had acquired a melodic
character, it had sounded its own death-knell. In
Bach's "trios"—the violin and viola da gamba sonatas
—the basso continuo was already forced to occupy an
insignificant place; and in the chamber and orchestral
music of the pre-Haydn period it disappeared for
ever.

A particularly important part in the reformation
of melodic structure was played by the vocal and
instrumental art of the seventeenth century. The old
vocal and instrumental embellishments were purely
ornamental, the mere trappings of the essential melody;
they were rarely expressive. In the new period, up
to the end of the eighteenth century, the delight in
improvised ornament was as active as ever, but a
good deal of the ornamentation became stylized,
without serious detriment to the basic melody. The
best and most individual madrigal-composers, however—Marenzio, Monteverdi, and others—had already
rescued their melodies from the caprice of singers (as
Bach did later in a higher degree) and devoted their
finest craftsmanship to providing their own embellishments; and in the same way the seventeenth century exerted itself to render its ornamentation expressive and to enlist melody and decorative invention
under the same banner. The continued endeavour to
achieve passionate utterance, sharp characterization,

and vivid tone-painting played a vital part in originating the modern motif.

These were the factors that gave the new style of composition its general character in the seventeenth century. There was no fundamental difference between sacred concerted music, secular chamber music (the cantata and duet), opera, oratorio, or even instrumental chamber music. The ideal that inspired all these forms was sung; and in this sense their development ran on identical lines. But the actual shapes they took were quite distinct. We may begin with the chamber cantata, since by its very nature it remained the most independent of external circumstances and, in addition to affording the purest example of the development of the seventeenth-century idea of form, provided composers with an experimental training-ground and the necessary equipment for opera and oratorio.

The cantata was a lyrical form in dramatic shape, a unique phenomenon akin to the modern ballad. Its particular manifestations showed no variety or individuality; as a form it was stereotyped and monotonous. Its natural emotion was not deep or heartfelt, but was expressed by superficial ornamentation. The pastoral, in its progress from the idyllic to the pathetic, remained its principal sphere, just as on the literary side it derived from the idylls of Theocritus and Virgil and Ovid's *Heroides*. The madrigal, both sacred and secular, had long before adopted a kind of narrative framework—later to be established as recitative—to which prominence was usually given by a homophonic treatment of the voices. Oddly enough, it was quite a long time before monody incorporated in the cantata the forms that had been at its disposal from the very first (the recitative-like madrigal and the air), or rather before it extracted from recitative the element of pure song and gradually made it independent. A characteristic of the cantata was the complete subordination of poetry to music, which quickly became established. In the sixteenth century the composer had regarded himself as the interpreter of the poet. Petrarch, Boccaccio, Sannazaro, and even Dante enjoyed a new popularity, thanks to the musicians; and Ariosto and Tasso were glorified in the settings of their verse. In monodic settings, too, the Florentines at least took poetry seriously. Caccini's musicianship was too weak to achieve anything more than conventional sentiment in the madrigal and modest grace in the song form. But a whole group of composers, with Monteverdi as their leader, aimed at truth and accuracy in the expression of emotion and did not shrink from employing any audacities of harmony or melody to attain their end.

The pursuit of this lofty ideal still required a definite poetic stimulus. But it was of short duration. Composers soon diverted their energies into a channel of sensuously beautiful melody, and for that they needed poetry that fitted most closely the musical forms they had won for their own. There arose an entirely new kind of *poesia per musica*, which lost in invention and content what it gained in flexibility and smoothness. This disjoined and unsound relationship between the sister arts at first gave the Italians the advantage, but later led to the impoverishment of their musical lyric and created that gap between folk-song and art-song which in German music was to be filled so wonderfully by the Lied. In Italy, however, this relationship was a practical necessity, since only on these lines was it possible to ensure normality in harmony and melody. In accordance, one might say, with the natural law of the conservation of energy, composers of cantatas and operas in the seventeenth century set aside conscious obedience to theoretical principles and devoted all their energies to writing music that obeyed its own laws.

The task that faced them was extraordinary and unprecedented. It was possible, of course, to borrow from folk-song and popular melody, and this was done to a greater or less degree. But on the whole the tendency was to move away from popular influences. The object was to establish quite independently the laws of pure monody from the structure of short themes to their combination in an elaborately articulated whole. The example of Florence was followed by Rome, where men like Mario Savioni, Luigi Rossi, Marc' Antonio Cesti and particularly Gacomo Carissimi cultivated the cantata with passionate devotion and enlarged its possibilities of expression by giving greater scope to pathos, grace, and humour—the last a specialty of the Roman school. Nowhere does the cantata show such abundant variety of form as in the work of the Roman composers, such versatility in the combination of arioso and recitative, such natural ease and fluency of style. The rondo cantata, however, in which there was a lively treatment of a recurring arioso section, may be regarded as the favourite form. Contemporary with the Roman school of cantata-composers and succeeding them were the masters of Venice and northern Italy, led by Bologna. The cantata with instrumental accompaniment owed its typical form, after much tentative experiment, to Alessandro Stradella of Modena; but the classical representative of the cantata's maturity in all its various forms and its most prolific composer was the Neapolitan Alessandro Scarlatti, who has left us in his cantatas an inexhaustible treasure of melodic invention and sensuous beauty. To him is due the definitive shape of the da-capo aria. In this form the claims of poetry are reduced to the most modest scale, so that music may as far as possible remain its own master and pursue its course unchecked. What the aria demanded of its text was simply the set form—principal section, middle section, repetition of principal section—a definite emotion, and nothing more unless it was a suggestion for a picturesque accompaniment, the object being to produce a kind of vocal sonata. In a later age, when naturalism was the vogue, it may have been regarded as a mistake that this vocal sonata should have been transplanted into opera; but the grandeur, richness, and fruitful possibilities of the form itself were demonstrated a hundred times over by Bach, Handel, Hasse, Jommelli, and Mozart.

The new style also took possession of the motet, which became the sacred cantata. If monody may be said to have brought emancipation to secular song, it threatened church music with a danger of which musicians of the time were fully aware. The evidence of that is the mass of church music in the old style, written by composers who were otherwise quite "modern"; and yet the right note was not truly struck. The sixteenth-century tradition survived most vigorously and most naturally at Rome, but Venetian composers like Antonio Lotti and Neapolitans like Alessandro Scarlatti also took a delight in conscious archaism. The age of innocence of a-cappella music, however, was over. The sacred cantata held the field and adapted itself readily enough, after a short florescence of monodic and concerted motets, to the forms of secular song, developing a tendency to abandon Biblical texts in favour of a fulsome religious poetry in the baroque manner. It was in the sacred cantata that the new relationship between vocal and instrumental parts developed and became firmly established. The concerted treatment of the parts in instrumental chamber music became the model for a similar treatment of vocal and instrumental parts in combination. In place of the merely ornamental contrasts of separate choirs to be found in earlier music, there prevailed from now on an ingenious and imaginative alternation of voices and instruments. The instrument anticipates the theme of the voice-part or develops it still further, and the parts interchange or combine with the utmost freedom and ease. Side by side with the creation of the small cantata came the establishment of the form on a large scale. The ornate Venetian church music became divided up into choruses and solo songs and readily embraced the new forms; the result was the "grand cantata," in which the claims of music involved the subjection even of the venerable text of the Mass itself. It was not in borrowed forms or in the use of instruments that the secularization of the church music lay, but in the change of standpoint, the naked subjectivity, the all too personal relation of the worshipper to the Deity. In the music of the sixteenth century God's answer to prayer had been implicit in the supplication, but now the suppliant himself appeared upon the scene.

The development of opera ran on similar lines to that of the cantata, except that here the conflicting claims of drama and music naturally could never be completely reconciled. In individual cases drama continually succeeded in re-establishing its rights, but unfortunately this was generally done by a vaguely idealistic re-creation of Greek tragedy; the approach was literary and hence one-sided, and there was no proper consideration of the part that music had a right to play. How insignificant in effect the supposed realization of such ideals could be was shown by the first phase of the new form's development. For all that its earliest exponents did to bring it to life, Florentine opera would have remained a bloodless phantom, a merely temporary adjunct to the festivities of the Grand Duke's court, had not a composer of genius, Cʟᴀᴜᴅɪᴏ Mᴏɴᴛᴇᴠᴇʀᴅɪ, at the time *maestro di cappella* to the Duke of Mantua, taken it in hand. The general structure of early opera was based on an entirely false conception, the engineer, the scene-painter, and the dancer being considered more important than the poet or the musician. In his *Orfeo*, produced at Mantua in 1607, Monteverdi showed for the first time that within this framework it was possible to create a living, passionate, intensely dramatic music. For the first time he allowed the instruments to speak a language of their own—though it is a mistake to assert that he already used them in the modern manner. He won a place in the drama for instrumental music, which it was to lose all too soon; and if all use he made of it was concentrated, it was for that reason all the more brilliant.

Arianna (1608) seems to have made an even deeper impression than *Orfeo*. All that has survived is the famous Lament of the deserted heroine, which for many years was accepted as a model of its kind —music of immortal verity and loveliness. The operas that followed *Arianna* are completely lost, with the exception of two works of the great master's old age—he had since become *maestro di cappella* at St. Mark's, Venice (1613)—which reveal a ripe mastery of characterization, melody, and form. Through all Monteverdi's work runs the dramatic impulse; its quickening fire is felt in his a-cappella madrigals and imparts a glow to the masterpieces of subjective inspiration that he wrote for church and chamber. In his *Combattimento di Tancredi e Clorinda*, performed in 1624, he produced the first example of a genuine secular oratorio, though he was not actively concerned with the creation of a new form and indeed only considered the single detail of a new device of instrumentation worth mentioning. In his lifetime Montervedi drew upon himself that hatred of the reactionaries which is the lot of genius. Even today no one can remain indifferent to the disturbing stimulus of his music. He is the greatest representative of a period of revolution in which the very foundations of tradition were shaken.

Florentine opera did not last long; and for that both circumstances and its own nature were responsible. It early won occasional acceptance in a number of Italian cities; but its first home that could in any sense be called permanent was in the cardinals' palaces in Rome. Here several important works were produced, in which the tendency was to abandon dramatic expression in favour of purely lyrical melody, under the powerful influence of the Roman cantata. Some of the opera librettos written by GIULIO ROSPIGLIOSI, poet and later Pope, have a particular historical importance, since they provided for the first time a contrast to the sentimental pathos of the principal characters in the figures of low comedy, such as the page and the nurse. This mixture of styles was popular throughout the seventeenth century, until antiquarian purism stepped in and restored to opera seria its exclusively pathetic character.

A Roman was the author of these works, and it was mostly Roman singers who supplied the opera for the first permanent theatre at Venice (1637). For many years after that, Venice remained the principal home of opera in Italy, and, for that matter, in Europe. At first it set an example to other cities and produced its own operas; later from the beginning of the eighteenth century, it continued, with its large number of public

theatres, to act as a consumer. Venetian opera swung
away more and more from the ideas of the first inven-
tors of the form. FRANCESCO CAVALLI, a pupil of Monteverdi, was the most influential of the Venetian composers. He was a master of subtle characterization, who
knew how to write recitative full of life and interest
and succeeded in producing scenes that were genuinely
dramatic and theatrically effective. But in the tender
and appealing work of the Roman composer Marc'
Antonio Cesti arioso was introduced into opera for
its own sake. The solemn overture of Monteverdi and
Cavalli was succeeded by the vivid, graphic, descrip-
tive sinfonia of about 1660, to be followed in turn
by the empty formality of the sinfonia of Venetian
opera in its decline. The chorus of the Florentine
operas became reduced to the insignificant interjections
of supernumerary characters and often disappeared
completely. Simple pastoral or mythological subjects
were replaced by heroic or historical themes, in which
the whole of ancient and early mediæval history
was garbled to provide an excuse for love-intrigues.
The librettist became the obsequious slave, first of the
stage engineer and then of the composer, while the
composer was more and more reduced to the role of
an obliging purveyor of material for the castrato and
the prima donna. Opera developed into a succession
of arias, the business of simulating some dramatic connexion between them being relegated to recitative.
A certain number of situations became stereotyped
—scenes of eavesdropping, mistakes of identity, out-
bursts of jealousy, dreams and conjurations—and
these continually offered a challenge to the skill of
rival composers. The librettist's technique consisted
in involving half a dozen pairs of lovers, with the
addition of an odd supernumerary, in all sorts of
entanglements and complications and then reconciling

them all at the end. Thus opera, considered as an artistic whole, degenerated gradually into an æsthetic monstrosity, and as time went on, the objections to which it laid itself open grew stronger. But, for all that, its composers achieved wonders, not merely from the musical but also from the dramatic point of view. To appreciate the achievement of baroque opera we must take the framework of its style for granted, admitting as inevitable in the circumstances the large part played by convention.

This proviso is particularly necessary in the case of the Neapolitan school, which with its founder, Francesco Provenzale, and especially with its leader, Alessandro Scarlatti (1659–1726), was to break the Venetian influence. Scarlatti's dramatic talent was slight, but he was a great composer with an inexhaustible fount of melody, and he was responsible for finally establishing the form of the operatic aria, to which he contributed an increasing refinement of ornamentation and elaborate instrumental accompaniment. He marks the point of departure for the development of opera in the eighteenth century.

Opera as represented by the style of the Venetian school enjoyed a triumphal progress throughout Europe. France and Germany pursued different paths, in accordance with their different political circumstances. In France Italian opera was at first imported without great attempt at adaptation or reconstruction. Cardinal Mazarin invited an Italian opera company to perform in Paris in 1645. This incursion was followed by others; and in the 1660's Paris made the acquaintance of two important works by Francesco Cavalli. Meanwhile, however, the poet Perrin and the composer Cambert, cunningly using the ballet de cour as a basis, had attempted to create a truly national opera; their *Pomone* (1671) was performed at

the opening of the newly founded "Académie de
Musique," which, significantly enough, had been
preceded about ten years before by a royal "Académie
de Danse." Circumstances were against Perrin and
Cambert, and their enterprise failed. A successor arose
who took over their work with better fortune. This
was GIAMBATTISTA LULLI, a Florentine, who basked
in the gracious favour of the "Roi Soleil," and created
the French heroic opera, with its two guiding stars
—Love and Glory. In the form that he originated,
with its magnificent array of dances and choruses,
its characteristic and more richly accompanied recitative, the concise melodic style of its ariosi, and—
most important of all—its continued, if only partial,
adherence to a certain principle of dramatic pro-
priety, it remained until the time of Gluck the shield
and buckler of tradition and the repository of a
jealously guarded style.

In England, too, opera began to take root in the
court masques, a survival and an imitation of the festival performances that were all the rage in Renaissance Italy, in which originally music had only the
modest task of supplying choral songs and accompaniments to the dances. The interpolation in Shakspere's
Tempest is a typical masque of the period. From these
masques there developed in the course of the seventeenth century a number of hybrid productions akin
to opera, among them a work that, allegedly, was
sung throughout—*The Siege of Rhodes* (1656), the
text of which was by Sir William Davenant. It is
difficult to say how it came about that England, where
the door was always open to Italian influences, never
created a national opera, as did Italy herself, France,
and eventually Germany. The reason may be not so
much a matter of history as of psychology and climate;
it is to be found, perhaps, in the difference between the

Italian and the English attitude towards music. Music is not the natural means of expression for the Englishman to the same extent as it is for the Italian. He regards it as something higher than a mere vehicle of the emotions and passions; and this explains why in England music remained in a subordinate position to drama. England produced instrumental pieces and ballets and created "supernatural" and "romantic" scenes; but, on the whole, English opera remained a "Singspiel," a spoken play with an abundance of complementary music. The actual musical life of England was to be found in the music that amateurs made for themselves in the home. Here the "fancy" was cultivated long after the rest of Europe had adopted the Italian concerted style and the virtuoso trio and solo sonata. The fancy, a polyphonic form written for the viol consort, had an intimate charm and attraction comparable only with that of the chamber music of the eighteenth century. HENRY PURCELL (1659–95), who wrote music for the theatre as well as an actual opera, was the last important creative force of a country which, as far as music is concerned, has since depended on foreign importations. Purcell may be compared to some extent with MOZART, not only on account of his tragically short career, but also because of the ease with which he assimilated foreign styles. He wrote trio sonatas in the Italian style; but in the strength of their melodic line they are still typically English, and so are his fancies, with their daring harmonic progressions. Besides his effective church music, which culminates in his magnificent *Te Deum*, his miniature opera *Dido and Æneas* stands on a pinnacle by itself, a model of pure and profound expression achieved by the most modest means.

In Germany the first growth of a national opera

was nipped in the bud. HEINRICH SCHÜTZ wrote for
the Saxon court in 1627 the first opera in German,
Dafne, which was undoubtedly in the spirit of Monteverdi. Later a number of German courts tried the
experiment of opera in the vernacular, not so much
in South Germany and Austria, where Munich and
Vienna both remained faithful to Italian opera, as in
the centre and the north—at Brunswick, Hanover,
and Weissenfels. At Brunswick there were two periods when German opera flourished, the second
associated with a distinguished name, GEORG KASPER
SCHÜRMANN. Dresden soon deserted to Italian opera
and remained faithful to it longer than any other
German city. The glories of Leipzig, Nuremberg,
and Augsburg pale beside those of Hamburg, where
for fifty years an operatic tradition was kept alive
which throws a melancholy light on the state of affairs in Germany at the time. There was a vague
idea prevalent that it was the function of opera to
be ennobling; and hence when the Hamburg opera
was founded, in 1678, its secondary object was to
provide edification and the first works produced were
on Biblical subjects. Soon there was a serious decline.
The operas became extremely crude and lost all consistency of style. German and Italian texts were
combined without scruple or hesitation, and all sense
of artistic and moral responsibility disappeared. Both
by the choice of language and by the spirit in which
the librettists approached their task German opera
was doomed to failure. A producer of genius like
the talented and enterprising JOHANN SIGISMUND
KUSSER could lend the tottering structure for a short
time the semblance of solidity; and a master of melody
and colour like REINHARD KEISER was able to support
it for several years. But in the end it was submerged
and overwhelmed by the tide of foreign affectation.

We shall see later how modest were the origins of truly national German opera, when at last the time was ripe for it.

For much the same reasons German song also deteriorated. The monodic movement from Italy might have led to a new growth of lyrical art if German poetry had been ready for it; but by the time it was able to provide musicians with the texts they wanted for the madrigal and the cantata the opportunity had passed. In the meantime the Thuringian composer HEINRICH ALBERT made tentative efforts to find suitable melodies for the strophic verses of the Königsberg poets; and what he aimed at and seldom achieved was brought to fulfilment by a master of song, ADAM KRIEGER. In these songs, which were adopted by students all over Germany, a wide range of emotions —from exuberant heartiness to youthful melancholy —found genuine and authentic expression. In the time of Albert and Krieger and later, a whole mass of utterly inferior ditties also became popular throughout the country. Their vogue did not, however, prevent musicians from feeling a pronounced contempt for strophic song—the basis of the Lied; indeed, it makes such an attitude comprehensible. German song declined still further at the end of the century with the growing tendency to adapt words to existing dance-tunes and instrumental melodies, generally of fashionable French origin. The aria and the cantata choked the growth of the Lied. Only German sacred song, which found in PAUL GERHARDT a true poet, was still the inspiration of genuinely musical talent.

Instrumental Music in the Seventeenth Century

In instrumental music monody achieved an even more
decisive victory of new over old than in vocal music.
The disintegration that followed its introduction was
more severe and the new edifice that it erected more
striking. The culminating-point, to which the development of the sixteenth century had led up, was Giovanni Gabrieli's orchestral sonata, the basis of which
was a concerted antiphony of contrasted masses of
tone—such as strings and brass—and the contrast
between sections consisting of contrapuntal imitation
for the finer-toned instruments and homophonic movements built up on mighty pillars of sound, in which
dance-rhythms were often employed and a strongly
accented triple time was favoured. This use of sonorous tutti in the manner of a ritornello was adopted
by Gabrieli from the canzon francese. A number of
Venetian and north Italian composers cultivated this
type of orchestral canzon for a short time, but it
soon lost its independent existence as an instrumental
form and dwindled to the short introduction to the
grand cantata. Its grave and solemn movements and
its use of the wind ensemble had a particular attraction for the German composers of church music and
cantatas.

In Italy, however, it took on a new lease of life
before it was finally submerged. The contrasted
upper parts of the two concerted groups—a violin
and a cornet, for example—were embroidered in the

most elaborate fashion with ornaments, runs, trills, and arpeggios. The virtuoso advanced his claim, and an individual, subjective character began to appear in music for festivals and state occasions. In this way there came into existence quite early, as if by accident, the primitive form of the concerto grosso, in which, between the unvarying repetitions of a ritornello for the tutti, individual instruments indulged in virtuosity to their hearts' content. This form, the combination of so-called "symphonies" with solo improvisations, was undoubtedly much cultivated in Venice and Rome. Its weakness was that in spite of all its simplicity it lacked unity, the unity that could be achieved only by thematic association and coherence of ideas. No wonder, then, that the Venetian orchestral sinfonia disappeared completely and carried on, so to speak, an underground existence until it finally came to light again at the end of the seventeenth century at Rome, Bologna, and Modena—cities that boasted particularly flourishing musical academies. By this time it was able to take advantage of the new clarification of harmonic relationship and the extraordinary progress in the conception of writing for instruments that had been made in chamber music. The concerto grosso had appeared.

This development had begun with the canzon francese and continued in an uninterrupted straight line to the creation of modern sonata form, the last and most mature form of pure instrumental music. The canzon francese already contained the undeveloped germs of what was to come; in it the contrasts of time, tempo, and texture which were essential for an organically constructed instrumental composition were already foreshadowed. The appearance of the basso continuo helped to sharpen these contrasts. At first, until about 1620, the canzon regarded

the continuo with suspicion, anxious as it was to
avoid being compelled to surrender its essentially
polyphonic character. Already, however, at this stage
the component parts of the work became detached
and took the form of separate, contrasted movements.
The result was a chequered pattern, made up of short
fughetta-like sections, dance-rhythms, and homophonic
movements characterized by gentle melancholy or
boisterous energy. "Capriccio" is the proper name for
this transitional form, which continued for a long time
to influence the composition of solo chamber music
and concerted works for a few instruments. It was
in this shape that the canzon was taken over by
FRESCOBALDI. He was not, however, content with it
as it stood; he felt a need for binding together at
least the principal movements of this complex whole
by means of thematic unity. In his works the theme
of the first movement undergoes ingenious transformations, which are quite often barely recognizable,
with different time-signatures and increasingly rapid
tempos; while between the principal movements come
free fantasies, serving as connecting links. Frescobaldi's
use of this principle of variation, which runs through
the whole of the instrumental music of the seventeenth
century, had a particular influence on the German
sonata-composers. To the neutral character of his
thematic material, which did not appeal to the newly
awakening taste for virtuosity, we must attribute the
fact that his immediate influence made itself felt more
strongly in compositions for clavier and organ than
in chamber music. Also the type of canzon that
aimed at developing the latent possibilities of a single
theme and led eventually to Bach's figure was soon
relegated entirely to clavier music; it was incompatible
with the art of the continuo.

At the same time the sonata for a few instruments

with continuo never entirely gave up imitative treatment, and its principal movement always implied a
grateful acknowledgment of its direct descent from
the canzon francese. It had, in fact, taken over the
lively imitations of the canzon and adapted them to
new conditions. Not, of course, that the old polyphony in four, five, or even six parts disappeared completely even in the Italian continuo sonata of the seventeenth century. The natural result of a greater number
of parts was a return to concerted music with contrasted groups of instruments, which paved the way
for the concerto grosso. However, the principal effect
the continuo had was to reduce the number of instrumental parts in the canzon. The small vocal concerto
provided the model for the instrumental duet, which
very soon secured general acceptance; it was usually
written for two violins with continuo accompaniment,
the bass being reinforced by another string instrument,
the viola da gamba or the violoncello. In this trio
sonata of the seventeenth century the strings gradually
ousted the wind. All this sonata literature is eminently
violin music, and it displays a very specific invention, which as time goes on grows more intense and
purer, inspired by the particular charm of the instrument. The contrasts of legato and spiccato are in
themselves almost a sufficient guide to the structural
divisions of the sonata. The string family became the
normal instrumental body, and in the relation between
strings and wind we have the first sign of their
arrangement in the modern orchestra.

In addition to these forms, which had their origin
in the canzon, the sonata also adopted new ones
whose principles were dictated by the continuo:
improvisation and variation. The continuo gave free
rein to virtuosity. Over long-sustained, slowly moving notes in the bass the sequence held high festival,

sometimes to the point of riotous excess, content at
first with empty formulas, but gradually developing
a more supple type of figuration. Over a constantly
repeated figure in the bass—the ostinato—composers
erected an elaborate edifice of variations, designed to
afford opportunities for a progressive show of virtuosity, the favourite culmination being a transformation
to rapid triple time. Such methods soon made it possible to blend the set of variations with the variations-
suite. The bass themes of variations of this kind, which
were originally songs or dance-tunes, were reduced
to pregnant harmonic formulas, thus forcing the
concerted parts to be more concise and laying on them
a heavier artistic responsibility. At the end of the
century the favourite type of variation form was the
chaconne, founded on a bass theme in triple time and
fixed rhythm.

From these various materials the early classical sonata was built up. The time of uncertainty and experiment passed extraordinarily quickly, and it was not
long before the development of the individual movements was achieved and a clear conception formed of
the appropriate outlines of the whole. Economy of
means made it necessary to take great pains in con-
structing the subjects of fugal movements and the
melodies of slow movements. One of the most striking
things in the history of instrumental music is the way
in which the blending of what may be called "neutral"
themes and brilliant figuration gave birth to the
flexible modern fugue-subject, with its strongly characteristic profile, and, inspired by the elegiac arioso
of the Roman and Venetian cantata, the instrumental
"cantabile" appeared. In the movements that were
treated contrapuntally the idea of imitation had, so
to speak, to be discovered anew. The trio sonata continued to cling to these movements, as a counter-

balance to the more superficial sections given up to
virtuosity. In them it found a reassurance against the
menace of dilettantism. In these "canzoni" (as the
more pretentious imitative movements of the sonata
continued to be called for quite a long time) attention
was always paid to craftsmanship. As in the later
chamber duet, it was regarded as a point of honour
to write in canon; the trio sonata rarely descended to
facile successions of thirds.

From the restless capriccio grew the "sonata da
chiesa" or church sonata, which in its simplest form
was based on a few simple contrasts expressed in the
form of two pairs of movements. Each pair consisted
of a slow and a quick movement; but to these were
added contrasts of time and structure between the
quick movements—one being in a more severe, the
other in a freer, style—and of key between the slow
movements. The decrease in the number of movements was accompanied by an increase in their scope
and intrinsic value, by a greater consistency of emotional content between different movements and a
more logical conception of the work as a whole. The
principle of the capriccio, one is tempted to suspect,
is to be found in a secret tendency towards program
music. The church sonata, on the other hand, became
in its purest form the most absolute music imaginable
—if indeed there is such a thing as absolute music. It
recalls the heroic atmosphere and elegiac mood of
Poussin's landscapes. Fond though it is of chromatic
themes, it restrains and sublimates all strong emotion.
In the noblest melody, in the purest euphony, it found
for the first time the laws of a cogent system of
modulation. The language that it speaks with such
restraint is not ours; yet this wealth of splendid music
can still grip our attention, can even charm us and lay
us under an enduring spell. For a whole century—

from 1650 to 1750—as long as the continuo maintained its vitality, the sway of the "sonata da chiesa" prevailed. The great names of its hey-day, which is associated with the churches and academies of Venice, Bologna, Modena, and Rome, were Legrenzi, Bassani, Vitali, and, above all, Corelli, dall' Abaco, and Handel; and Tartini and Gluck still paid it homage.

Beside the church sonata came the "sonata da camera" or chamber sonata, a succession of dance-movements with or without a freely constructed introductory movement. The idealized dance existed as early as the sixteenth century, and the oldest printed collections of dances for lute, keyboard instruments, or strings already show us not only individual movements of considerable melodic charm, often with variations, but also successions of typical dance forms, knit together by a less rigid principle of variation—in other words, the origins of the suite. In Italy the incentive offered by the dance was directed to the service of chamber music and the concerted and monodic styles, and, just as in Germany, the variations-suite was cultivated as well as the succession of independent dance-movements. The composition of the suite changed in accordance with the constant reaction of the dance itself to new influences, principally French. About 1660, mainly through the example of the French lutenists and the clavier composers who followed in their footsteps, a stock succession of movements became established, in which the rhythmic life of the dance found its ideal expression. These were the sober allemande, the brisk courante, the slow and melancholy sarabande, and the lively gigue. Between the sarabande and the gigue it was usual later on to insert the little characteristic dances, which became fashionable through the French dancing-masters' insatiable passion for novelty—the minuet, passepied, rondeau, bourrée, gavotte, and the rest. In Italy, where the inclination towards chamber music was so strong, these dances became stylized, which made it easier for them to merge into the movements of the church sonata. The allemande would take the place of the canzon, and the sarabande that of the slow second movement. The intrusion of the lighter types of dance-movement led eventually to the church sonata's having to exchange its first home for the secular music-room. For that matter, the Church from the beginning of the eighteenth century demanded music more elaborately scored and more splendid in effect —the full panoply of the orchestra.

In Germany it was different. There the dance-movement and the suite were only united to the continuo after some difficulty. There was a reluctance to give up polyphony, and the bright boisterous wind instruments were preferred to the aristocratic violin. The result was open-air rather than chamber music. The same composers who extended so enthusiastic a welcome to the Italian dance-song produced in their dance-movements the healthiest, the most popular, the most characteristically German music imaginable. The growing influence of the South affected the stability of the German suite. The gay pieces for wind instruments, intended for performance in the open air, suffered least. Their joyous irresponsibility is seen at its best in the engaging "tower sonatas" (music to be played from the towers of churches and other public buildings) written at the end of the century by men like PETZEL and REICHE. Just when the German suite stood at the parting of the ways between chamber and orchestral music Lulli came to the rescue with his ballet suite. The Germans reacted gladly to this new stimulus.

The reason is not far to seek. The Lullian suite,

with its five-part writing which treated even the lowest instruments as individuals, could be linked up with the tradition of the old variations-suite. Moreover, it was admirably suited to the new home of the suite, the middle-class and student collegia musica, whose members were anxious to have something for their fingers to do and thoroughly enjoyed taking an active part in music that was full of substance and energy. At the same time Lulli's opera overture—the "French" overture, as it is called—became the normal introductory movement of the German suite, after successive attempts had been made to adopt the intrada, the canzone, and the Italian sinfonia in the form of the capriccio or the Venetian opera symphony. There was once more genuine orchestral music. In addition to the body of strings concerted parts were also written for wind instruments, either the two oboes and bassoon of Lulli's trios or—better still—two trumpets (clarini), which emphasized the popular character of this type of music-making. For nearly fifty years the "ouverture," as the ballet suite was christened after its introductory movement, was the favourite music of the German collegia. The best composers produced examples of the form, containing a rich store of healthy and joyous melody. Some, such as Kusser, Erlebach, Georg Muffat, and J. K. F. Fischer, attached themselves more closely to the French model and, like the minor French composers, continued to draw inspiration from the stage and dances of the day. Others, among them Bach and also Telemann, Fasch, and Förster, made the form a vehicle for music of wider range and greater depth. At the same time the new enthusiasm for orchestral music was an aid to the pure development of German chamber music. The organists and town musicians of North Germany, influenced partly by the Italians and partly by the

English, took a particular interest in the trio sonata—with this difference, however, that instead of two violins they preferred to write for violin and bass viol (viola da gamba). Thanks to the bass viol, which was peculiarly the virtuoso instrument of the North, they indulged more than the Italians in variation and fantasy.

Instrumental monody—the solo sonata—had the hardest task. The sixteenth-century tradition that it had to build upon consisted principally of a riotous luxuriance of ornamentation. This had taken two forms—the coloratura treatment of a vocal melody and the variation of dance-tunes; but in neither case was there as yet any notion of organic principles of melody. The vehicle of the new instrumental monody was not at first a primarily melodic instrument, such as the violin or cornet, but one whose natural function was to play a bass part—the bass viol. For this there were very good reasons. With its large number of strings and aptitude for rapid movement, it was, like the lute, naturally suited to be the instrument of virtuosity. Already in the sixteenth century, in Spain, Italy, and particularly England, it was much used for improvisation, the favourite form being the varying of a short bass theme, possibly taken from a song- or dance-melody. It had also adopted from the lute the practice of playing chords and presenting the semblance of polyphony, and this enabled it to combine melody and accompaniment in the most ingenious and suggestive manner. In England the bass viol was still cultivated at a time when the violin was triumphing everywhere else, just as the elegant "fancy" remained popular after the rest of Europe had given a welcome to a more brilliant concerted style. CHRISTOPHER SIMPSON's *Division Violist* (1659) was the classic instruction-book for English players. It was more than a mere technical treatise; it was rather a dignified school of improvisation and of all the forms in which that art was exercised. The bass-viol style of playing formed the foundation of the violin sonata, which inherited from it the partiality for embroidering a bass with brilliant runs, arpeggios, and other embellishments. From the bass viol the violin also acquired its love of variation, as well as its readiness to abandon the continuo and build up a polyphonic structure out of its own resources. The tradition of this style was preserved for many years in the German violin sonata. We owe to it the marvels of Bach's unaccompanied sonatas and partitas.

In Italy, too, composers began by transferring the canzon and the fugue to a solo instrument and assigned an increasingly important place in the violin sonata to the movement that represented an extract from a polyphonic composition. Corelli in his epoch-making Op. 5 (1700) handed on to the eighteenth century the form of the fugue, in which the majority of the parts were entrusted to the solo instrument. TARTINI, too, in a great number of his sonatas helped the instrument in this way to attain its ascendancy. The best balance between the two partners in the solo sonata is probably to be found in the work of ANTONIO VERACINI and EVARISTO FELICE DALL' ABACO. These composers succeeded in dividing equally between the two parts the harmonic material of a fugal movement with one or two subjects. After dall' Abaco there appeared the solo sonata with clavier obbligato. The duties of the accompanist became more and more responsible and it was no longer safe to leave his share to the accidents of improvisation. The second half of the eighteenth century may in fact be said to have been the age of the clavier sonata with a more or less obbligato part for the violin. All that remained open to the violin as a solo instrument, apart from the concerto, was the study.

The solo sonata, in common with the trio sonata, made use of several forms; but the one that had a particular importance in its history was the first movement of the chamber sonata, which was in two sections. Its origin was the allemande, but as time went on, it showed less and less trace of its ancestry in a dance form. Contrasts in its melodic structure appeared quite early. An idea would be stated and answered, the contrast being generally between the flowing legato melody natural to the allemande and elaborate figuration in the virtuoso style. It was in this form that the new principles of instrumental cantobile were first established. In the first half of the eighteenth century there was a continual increase in the length of movements and in the emphasis laid on contrast; the widely accepted transformation of the style of the concerto to the solo sonata was a sign of the times. The spans and stresses of the rising edifice grew more ambitious, until finally the last vestiges of the old style were thrown aside; the moving bass and the restrictions of a definite metrical scheme lost their binding force. The early classical sonata discovered sonata form for its first movement; and with the discovery of the form came a new spirit—the "dramatic" spirit of modern music.

At the end of the seventeenth century the grand orchestral sonata also reappeared in a particular form which was rich in possibilities for the future— the concerto grosso and the solo concerto. The name "concerto grosso" was first applied to the orchestral sonata; but the term also included the church sonata and later the chamber sonata with massed strings, so that "concerto" in this case referred to the method of performance. But the name also described a particular formal structure; and from the first quarter of the seventeenth century it was used exclusively in this sense. In the concerto grosso a number of characteristic effects of contrast were brought to life and fitted together in a properly adjusted whole. The old delight in pitting different blocks of instrumental tone against one another was revived in the form of a strongly marked contrast between a ritornello for full orchestra and a concertino for solo instruments. In Italy the concertino was generally written for two violins and violoncello, but the Germans preferred various solo wind instruments. This contrast between the forte of the tutti and the fainter sound of the solo instruments gives us a clear idea of the simple conception of musical dynamics that prevailed at the time. There was a further contrast between the simple melodic character of the ritornello and the impetuous virtuosity of the solo sections.

In the trio sonata and the solo sonata of this period the contrast between plain melody and its elaborate transformation by virtuosity had not yet been perfectly adjusted; and this is true even of Corelli's famous Op. 5. In the concerto grosso this contrast found at last its legitimate home and its æsthetic justification. The statement of the theme by the full orchestra, then contention and rivalry, assent or contradiction, on the part of the solo instruments, interruption and prolongation, digression or return to the starting-point, subordination of the orchestra to the soloist or the group of soloists—all this gave the concerto's three movements such intense vitality, such a wealth of new associations, that it is not surprising that from Italy it quickly passed to Germany and England and carried all before it. Practically all the streams of instrumental composition in the seventeenth century flowed into the concerto grosso; but a special contribution was made by the Venetian opera overture with its trumpet solos and by Lulli's overture and chaconnes, in which short compact episodes and variations were entrusted to a wood-wind trio. ARCANGELO CORELLI seems to have followed a different line of approach. The wealth of musical resources in Rome and a natural inclination to give his virtuosity wider scope may have led him consciously to combine the old ritornello symphony and the trio sonata. The immortal service that he rendered to music was the significant incorporation of the several parts in an essentially artistic whole.

The solo concerto appeared later than the concerto grosso. In the work of its first important exponent, the Bolognese composer GIUSEPPE TORELLI, the form is still primitive; the solo instrument is merely used to relieve the tutti and deals with the same material. As it developed, however, along the path that led to Tartini and Viotti, the combination of rival elements became more and more dramatic and the alternation of solo and tutti was dictated less by considerations of structure and tone than by an artistic impulse governing the whole.

The concerto grosso became the favourite instrumental form of the period. Composers, players, and listeners were all infatuated with it. Soon the resources it employed were multiplied, in accordance with the tendencies of the baroque period, and there was a return to the more massive structure of the old choral style. Alternatively the possibilities of tone-painting were exploited, as in the work of ANTONIO VIVALDI. The purest and noblest memorials of the Italian style are Handel's concerti grossi; of the German, with its greater variety and characteristic inflections, Bach's "Brandenburg" concertos, though their

individuality and wealth of dynamics and expression
take them far beyond the limits of the mere type. In
the second half of the eighteenth century the concerto
grosso declined, while the solo concerto continued
to flourish. From the dissolution and decay of the
older ideal the new symphonists took the materials
with which, after a momentous period devoted to
chamber music, they were to build their edifice.

Protestant Church Music

It is the glory of a few great and many lesser, devoted, humble Protestant masters that German music
in the seventeenth century did not wholly merge into
the stream of forms from Italy. Protestant sacred
music had first of all to define its relation to the new
instrumental style; here as in the Italian motherland the
old persisted vigorously beside the new. It did so
chiefly in the sumptuous Venetian motet forms, with
their many voices and many choirs, whose most tem-
peramental and colour-loving exponents were MICHAEL
PRAETORIUS and JOHANN HERMANN SCHEIN. Praetorius
revelled in the wealth of opportunity they afforded for
vocal and instrumental settings, and sought to bind
them with the chorale-melody in Florentine finery.
The north Italian influences were developed with
more independence, energy, and imagination by the
St. Thomas cantor, Schein, in his choral motets,
charged with overflowing strength, and his sacred
concertos, with their richly contrasting patterns. Beside the large-scale motets with their demand, too,

for an important body of instrumentalists, which had retained an extraordinary vitality, went the modest vocal motets for choirboy service—models at the same time for more rural use—in which the minor Thuringian cantors especially have handed down a treasury of simple yet full-sounding music, music homely and popular, yet reflective and filled with the genuine polyphonic spirit.

The master who sought to win a place in German church music for the new monodic, concerted music originating in the South was HEINRICH SCHÜTZ (1585–1672), one of the greatest German composers. The chorale played an unimportant part in his work; he made it his mission to win for his nation and creed dramatic music in all its true forms. He was twice in Italy, first as a personal pupil of Giovanni Gabrieli, then as a spiritual disciple of Monteverdi. From 1617 till the end of his life he was active at the Dresden court chapel. After a decade happily spent in organization, he toiled to check the effects, so fatal to art, of the Thirty Years' War. Three times he attempted to escape by travelling to Denmark. At the end of his long life, tired out, he willingly handed over the reins to the Italians, who were becoming more and more favoured in Dresden. This man of deep inwardness of character and tender sensibility, destined to live in a stormy age and isolated in his career and in his work, is of all artists one of the most moving, most ideal figures. He was well aware of the danger of dilettantism inherent in monody and issued warnings against it verbally and in three great publications of different character, in which he pointed to the permanent worth of the pure a-cappella style, and thus helped to ensure that the German composers down to Bach should never, like the Italians, have to keep it artificially alive.

Otherwise he accepted the new forms both enthusiastically and deliberately and sought to mould them
to the character of the German language and infuse
them with German warmth. In accordance with his
two visits to Italy, one part of these works has affinities with Gabrieli's music in the splendid drive
of its vocal and instrumental style—in this way
Schütz perfected for Germany the model of the
great free church cantata—and the other the music
of Monteverdi and Alessandro Grandi. Out of the
spirit of monodic song, the sphere of small vocal and
instrumental media and their combination with choir
and orchestra, there grew a wealth of ingenious,
expressive forms. There is in this music a sense of
springlike awakening, a continuous stirring of dramatic
life. From the motet grew the oratorio *scena;* and
in late old age, after many other attempts in the
oratorio style, Schütz wrote down his conception of
the dramatic rendering of the Passion in three separate
settings. Here, as always, his expression was of the
keenest, not shrinking from the most daring resources
of harmony and melody, yet always very simple and
genuine. In his urge towards the utmost truth of expression, in his aversion to all surface polish for the sake of
mere formal beauty, and at the same time in the instinctive sureness of his construction, Schütz, here where he is
greatest, is comparable only to a great German painter
—Albrecht Dürer.

Schütz's Faustian spirit was not inherited by any
of his imitators and pupils, not even by Andreas
Hammerschmidt—by virtue of his suave, attractive
melody the most influential among them—whose
ingenious *Dialogues* were the favourite form of religious music. The variety and fluency of Schütz's
forms suffered a limitation to a small number of fixed
formal types, to a more traditional way of handling

the relationship between voice and instruments. At
the same time there were in comparison with the
Italian cantata a few distinguishing features. The
favourite voice of the Italians was the soprano, of
the Germans the bass. Furthermore, in the German
cantata the instrumental part is far more exuberant.
There is no limit to the number of ritornellos and
sinfonias.

But in one respect Schütz's contemporaries enor-
mously enriched the church cantata, increasing its
content both in form and in poetic expression by
their use of the chorale. Through the chorale a piece
of mediæval Netherland tradition, which might otherwise not have survived so long, was rescued for a
later age. But the difference between the employment of the Gregorian and the Protestant chorale is
nevertheless great. Through its compact, popular form,
through its long exercise as congregational song, the
Protestant chorale had attained a purer crystallization
than the Gregorian had ever done. It had become not
merely the liturgical but also the poetic kernel of
church music. It was never to be used as a mere
connecting link, to disappear from the artistic whole;
whenever it emerges it does so as a living organism,
always drawing attention to itself as a symbol of the
universal and the divine. That this came to pass is
to the credit of the German organists who understood
Samuel Scheidt's decisive achievement and did not let
it pass unheeded.

The organ assumed an ever greater importance in
public worship. A second work of SCHEIDT, dating
from 1650, testifies to one of its functions, that of
accompanying congregational singing with the melody
unaltered, while giving prominence and life to the
subsidiary voices—a challenge to the profoundest
harmonic interpretation, which no one before Bach

was able fully to meet. Another of the organ's functions was to play the Magnificat responses, in which the dependence on liturgical motives and respect for the church modes—originally insisted upon —diminished more and more, so that eventually they were developed into a kind of school of fugue, with completely free thematic treatment. A third function was the elaboration of the chorale during Communion and the playing of preludes and postludes when hymns were sung by the congregation. In the course of all this the chorale was treated in every conceivable way. Variations could be made upon it, perhaps for home use on the clavier; the theme of the first line could be worked fugally, or the melody ornamented and introduced over a ground bass; or—and this was the ideal way—the simple melody could be both contrasted with and related poetically to the contrapuntal imitation of the subsidiary voices.

Most influential in this connexion was the work of JOHANN PACHELBEL of Nuremberg, whose education and widespread activities made him—like Gabrieli and Sweelinck previously—one of the most important disseminators. He was the chief representative of the South German style of organ-playing, with its highly varied treatment of the chorale and close connexion with the liturgy. The North German masters, with VINCENT LÜBECK and DIETRICH BUXTEHUDE at their head, turned rather to freer forms. They expanded the toccata, the fantasia, the capriccio, and the ricercar and filled them with imaginative content, while their attitude towards the chorale was more subjective and, one might almost say, less respectful.

What was suitable to the chorale on the organ was suitable also in vocal music. It was introduced into the new free concerted motets as a symbol of

the divine—as comfort, admonition, and promise—
and in contrast to the human. The text had become
in the course of time so intimately bound up with
the melody that the chorale played by instruments
alone could find a still more subtle and artistic employment and express a still profounder meaning.
An old, yet new, polyphonic music, suggestive of
the early motets, came to light again; only what had
once been meaningless combination was now instinct
with poetry. This poetical treatment of the chorale
was applied to all the new examples of concerted
motets which arrived from Italy with every fresh
generation of composers. It remained also when, about
1700, some of the German church-cantata librettists,
who had hitherto contented themselves with chorale
and Biblical texts, or at the most with strophic songs
on a small scale, introduced the great, free lyrical
forms of the Italians—the recitative and the aria.
Whereas Schütz had already stood for an exclusively
musical approach, there now arose sacred music of the
most subjective kind; and it was only natural that,
especially in pietistic circles, sharp opposition should
have been aroused by this operatic treatment of the
divine service. In point of fact, Bach alone succeeded
in so sublimating the baroque spirit of this style of
church music that down to this day even the most
susceptible have hardly been able to object to the use
of contemporary secular sources in his art.

Bach

What is there not to be found in the Bach cantata, sacred or secular! There are the grand Italian aria for one or more voices, accompanied by a simple continuo or by several instruments, the arioso, the recitative. There are choral motets, homophonic or fugal, there are concerted choral movements with the richest alternations of chorus and soli. The treatment of the chorale-melody exhausts possibility, from the plainest four-part harmonization upwards. In the introductions the orchestral symphony is represented from its earlist Gabrielian shape to the contemporary French overture, and on to the modern concerto form. All these things the greatest of musicians welded in that spiritual and melodic furnace which was Bach's and Bach's alone, into such a unity that the problems of style presented by his tentative predecessors in their essays to balance vocal and instrumental elements sink into nothingness.

Bach was a great river into which all things flowed; and all that his own age and the ages before him had done and dreamed of were his tributaries. That old polyphonic language that was his was in his generation not commonly to be found in this strength and naturalness; it was the outburst of waters from long-hidden springs. Symbolic is Bach's origin in the heart of Germany, sprung of a family of organists and town-bandsmen, then the most musical section of German society. In a family circle of relations by blood and

relations by art, near and far, he found the first
sustenance for a mind greedy for learning. He began
in the field of clavier music and of the motet and
cantata. He went on to the organ school of Pachelbel
and Buxtehude. Nothing that France or Italy could
provide in the way of stimulus but was eagerly ap-
prehended; not a stone was rejected, but every available one was put to an apt purpose in the building of
his art. He delighted in kindling this imagination at
alien fires; themes from foreign lands attracted him.
He would take up whole compositions by other composers and with his own more vigorous breath inspire
them with new life. His passacaglia would not have
existed without Buxtehude; nor the *"Forty-Eight"*
(*Das wohltemperirte Clavier*), had it not been for an
opuscule, *Ariadne Musica* (1715), by a gifted harpsi-
chordist, J. K. F. Fischer; nor his harpsichord suites
without the preparatory work done in that vast field
by the French. But he could touch nothing that did
not grow under his hand to the utmost completeness
and grandeur. All things flourish with him like the
trees of the forest, broad-crowned and superb, and
inevitable alike in the grandest branching polyphony
and the most delicate of melodic sprays and blossoms.
His polyphonic habit of thought led him along harmonic ways that, while not unlawful, were yet of the
utmost daring. He was first to make free and assured
use of the possibilities of equal temperament (the
division of the octave into twelve equal semitones,
which had been effected finally and definitely by
his contemporary Andreas Werckmeister), by com-
pleting the cycle of keys.

The art of the Bach cantata is an exposition of the
foundations and principles of the Christian faith,
and none more searching or more inexorable, deeper
or more precise has ever been. The temporal life and

the eternal, works and faith, mortality and death, sin and repentance, suffering and salvation—all the emotions and inspirations of the Christian soul exalted this, the greatest of preachers since Luther, not to theological abstractions, but to a passionate presentation by symbolic means of an incomparably vivid musical imagination. Bach's cantatas are truly a musical *biblia pauperum*. Joyous he could be, no man more so, as countless pages of his instrumental music show; but in the depths of his nature he was preoccupied with the mystery of man's end and the soul's yearning for redemption. A mystical rapture seizes him at the thought of the body's doom and the soul's hereafter.

Only in recent times has the world begun to apprehend Bach's unique musical imagination aright. So searching was his vision that his themes tell us unmistakably the conception he formed of the attributes of God the Father, of Christ as Lord, Redeemer, and Victor, of the Devil as tempter, serpent, and adversary. It is not that his imagination is a storehouse of ready-made motifs; rather is it the universe of a supreme creative power, crowded with the vital forms of his begetting. And it is not that his musical symbolism is primarily dependent upon the text. While the themes of his choral fugues and motets are marvels of concentrated eloquence and spirit, mysteriously inexhaustible, his recitative (which has practically nothing in common with the Italian secco) incomparably unites a free and precise verbal expression with rhythmic decision, a wealth of music and formal strength. It is a whole, not a complement. As for the Bach aria, it is monumental entity, yet filled with passionate thought and capable of the utmost flexibility.

And he, the most subjective and personal of polyphonic composers, felt more strongly than any other of his cantata-writing contemporaries the right of the chorale to the central place in his work. Hardly one of the two hundred cantatas that have come down to us is without its chorale; if in no other form, at least as a simple conclusion, with wonderfully expressive harmonies, to give as it were in the most concentrated form an ideal representation of the community. The symbolic outline of the hymns appears in movements of apparently the freest construction. Bach's favourite form in his chorale cantatas (about a quarter of the whole were solo cantatas) is a kind of adaptation of the chorale prelude, in which the objective hymn, sung in the treble, is set off by the more subjective utterances of the lower voices and the orchestral commentary. The rhetorical effects obtained by a show of increasing animation play no part in the Bach cantatas. Here the mere statement of the hymn, following upon a brilliant movement, declares by its very plainness the depth of its significance. Intensity, in those of Bach's greater works that were conceived as a whole, is achieved by the sheer weight of the matter of the music and its inevitable development. Nowhere, it may be said, is Bach the man seen to be more radically possessed than in these works: the festal *Magnificat* and the two surviving examples of his Good Friday music which treat of the Passion and Death of Jesus—the *Passion according to St. Matthew*, a communal drama of a compassion all-comprehending and an intuition unapproachable, and the *Passion according to St. John*, an absorbed contemplation of the mystery of the divine person of Christ. Finally, in the *Mass in B minor* Bach miraculously realized all that was most complete, comprehensive, and objective in his conception of the essence

and being of Christianity. Supreme musicianship, the
utmost vividness of imagination, and the profoundest
capacity for emotion were in Bach made one.

His instrumental music ranges over a perhaps still
wider spiritual field. Also in this field he epitomizes
the centuries and the nations. It is as though the
seventeenth-century Italians had only striven to develop all instrumental forms while leaving perfection
for him; it is as though François Couperin, the great
master of the harpsichord, and himself the completion
of the work of three generations, had developed the
French clavier suite to a high point only in order to
give Bach a stimulus. Part of this side of his work,
too, was dedicated to the Church. Those eminently
programmatic compositions, the chorale preludes, in
whose narrow room life lives at its utmost intensity,
give us the range of his feeling, as likewise does the
superb architecture of the organ preludes and fugues,
which are also program music, generally devotional in
content. But who shall tell the wealth of this man's
mind, revealed in the sparkling life of the orchestral
suites, in the concertos, in the intimate utterance of his
chamber sonatas, in the countless works of every sort
with which he endowed the domestic keyboard instruments—toccatas, preludes, fugues, variations, partitas,
and suites! Every instrument that was capable of
polyphonic expression received his outpourings. To
the harpsichord he makes a present of the Reincken
chamber sonata, the "Italian concerto," the new solo
sonata. The violoncello is set to play suites; proud
fugues and the mighty *Chaconne* are entrusted to
four fiddlestrings. He experiments; he makes a mixture
of all kinds of forms—and out of it emerges as a
matter of course a perfect shape. Bach's fugue is the
consummation of the species. His theme is always an
unmistakable individual in a definite situation, a crea-

ture born to experience; and its experiences correspond to its character. Hence no two fugues are alike in form, though all are consummate in their various ways. If that art whose spiritual content is the most concentrated has the best prospect of a long life, then will the inventions and sinfonias, and the preludes and fugues of the *"Forty-Eight"* endure for ever. The works of the last phase, the *Musical Offering* and *The Art of Fugue*, belong to what Goethe called "the supreme works of art which are frankly unprepossessing; they are ideals, which can and should be only approximately pleasing—æsthetic imperatives." Bach is of the company of those masters with whom every age and every individual must arrive at a new understanding; and still his greatness has not been appraised, nor can be ever.

Handel

Handel's greatness rests on quite other foundations than Bach's. The childish observation has been made that Handel wrote a heap of indifferent works which Bach had too thorough a training and too simple an eye to pure music to do; and this has brought upon him the misunderstanding of sciolists and even of masters. But Bach himself, Mozart, and Beethoven thought otherwise; and indeed Handel, if we take his personality as a whole, stands as little below Bach as Bach is below him. He was one of those musicians who only late in life discover and embrace their true vocation. Like Bach he ripened early; but while

Bach undertook those journeys—the farthest of them
to Hamburg—in which he learned his art, only in
order to enrich his mind and then to retreat again
into himself, Handel felt impelled, both as a musician
and as a man, to grow continually in breadth and
freedom. Hamburg first, then Italy—opening out to
his sturdy, healthy German musicianship as the school
of pure, true, classical melody—and finally England;
these are fixed as the stations in the upward climb of
a heroic life. And his exceptional productivity, in
instrumental works, in church music in the grand
manner, and in opera—he wrote about thirty Italian
operas for London—was the preparatory school for
his own particular creation, oratorio.

Oratorio had, when it came into Handel's powerful grasp, already had a long and interesting history.
As originally conceived, it was the means which the
Roman Counter-Reformation had specifically adopted
to combat the seductive lure of secular art and to
defeat it with its own weapons, by employing it in
the church for devotional purposes. It might use
Italian words or the rather more solemn tone of Latin,
but in either case it took over all the forms of secular
art that were current in the sixteenth and seventeenth
centuries—in historical order, frottola, villanella, canzonetta, madrigal, and solo cantata or choral cantata,
large or small. Its subjects, inherited from the age-old
mystery plays, were the stories and episodes of the Old
and New Testament and the legends of the saints.
These it set in a framework of two parts comprising
the edifying message, and connected them at first by
narrative, but afterwards gave them dramatic form. In
Carissimi's hands it had burgeoned as a Latin choral
work, but by Handel's time it had blossomed into
Italian oratorio, and as such had become a substitute
during Lent for the opera and its solo work. The

characteristics that distinguished the oratorio style
from the operatic lay in the appeal to the hearer's
imagination, in the incentive to, and the justification
for, a more delicate moulding of the musical material,
and especially in the more extended use of the chorus.

The way in which Handel met the claims of oratorio
is to be explained, not historically, but only by the
native sway of his whole mood and musical personality. About half of his oratorios, eighteen of them
perhaps, are dramas of imagination. Taking the Jewish
nation as his instance, he follows the fortunes of a
chosen people, he depicts their champions and their
adversaries; and he does this with a greatness and
simplicity, with a variety of detail and a pictorial
grasp, at times, too, with a sense of humour, that
argue alike the great musician, the great dramatist,
and the great man. The Florentine dream of the
renascence of classical drama here comes true. A
Greek would probably at once have understood the
position and the meaning of the chorus in Handel's
oratorio. The two oratorios which have done most to
establish his fame, *Israel in Egypt* and *Messiah*, stand
apart. *Israel*, that mighty choral oratorio, shows how
a people of God lives and grows in history. *Messiah*
dispenses entirely with action and resolves every event
into emotion, and in that way shows how the promises
of Christianity are fulfilled. The two together con-
stitute a free confession of religious faith comparable only to that of Bach's B minor Mass, which had
been completed but a short time before.

Great as is the sheer musical power that is shown
everywhere in these works, especially in the choruses,
which achieve the mightiest effects with the simplest
means, it is not there that we look for the full import
of Handel's creations. There can be no greater mistake
than to fancy that the oratorio was nourished on

ecclesiastical ground. On the contrary, it ranks with the opera as a free artistic effort, for in it for the first time a great artistic personality is speaking to his ideal public, to a nation and not to a parish. Handel's achievement is the preparation for what Beethoven afterwards did with the symphony; and it is on this eminence that these two masters, so utterly unlike, meet as conquerors. The performances of Handel's oratorios, particularly of *Messiah*, first in the British Isles and then in Germany, invigorated the whole of musical public life; they enfranchised art and addressed it to the world at large instead of to the narrow circle of connoisseurs.

MODERN TIMES

Homophony

BACH and Handel, composers of true polyphonic mettle, project, in their latest works, into a period that had long followed other ideals. The age of the figured bass ends in the triumph of homophony. As early as 1737 a champion of the moderns, Johann Adolp Scheibe, had stigmatized Bach's music as turgid and confused; and Jean-Jacques Rousseau gave even more one-sided expression to the spirit of the times when he advocated the cult of melody and turned his back on any harmonic solidity and still more on any counterpoint. Great was the decline from the native strength of the overtures of composers such as Bach and Fasch to the symphonic output of Italians or Italianate Germans, from the sonatas of Corelli or Abaco to those of Nardini or Pugnani with their feminine endings, their repetitions that protracted without enhancing, their windy effeminacy, their impotence in expression, and their substitution of noise for vigour. The change of taste can be read in their basses. These had once been part of the thematic structure, but now they move inconsequently in support of the harmonies with unwilling feet, at the most enlivened by subdivision into idle semi-quavers. With that, all melodic expression evaporated in endless *fioriture*.

We are now in the classical age of instrumental and vocal virtuosity, for which, however necessary as a brilliant school of melody, the historians have hardly had a good word. They found their scape-goat in Neapolitan opera as it developed after the death of Alessandro Scarlatti. Neapolitan opera had, indeed, abandoned itself with so little reflection to the lure of purely sensuous melody and done such violence to any kind of dramatic truth that the real motive for change came from within. JOHANN ADOLPH HASSE, the man of the moment, who set the librettos of Zeno and Metastasio to the entire satisfaction of Italy and Germany, had now reached the limit of what could be achieved by that tenderness and grace that came to him by nature. His greatest successor in the operatic field, NICCOLO JOMMELLI, who followed him in European favour, refined his orchestral accompaniment by an extended range of expression. In its *accompagnato* the orchestra seized upon the moments of passionate crisis in the recitative before the aria begins, and therein taught itself a hitherto unsuspected versatility, while the aria itself enlarged its repertory of forms. From the early years of the eighteenth century æsthetic theory took a lively interest in all operatic problems. Debate grew heated on the relative merits of the two national operas, Italian and French; recourse was had to classical drama in order to reach a genuine and independent conception of what opera should be. French opera showed itself impervious to any influences from the South, and attained, under its greatest master, RAMEAU, alone, within the limits of its traditional style, a refined and stable culture; whereas an Italian, TRAETTA, sought to unite the beauties of both operas.

The real reform of opera came from CHRISTOF WILLIBALD GLUCK, a master who, like Archimedes with his spiral, found his point of leverage outside what could strictly be called music and whom his enemies accordingly accused of making music without music. For this he called to his aid a man of fine intellect, whose instincts were æsthetic rather than poetical: Ranieri da Calzabigi. Gluck's actual achievement was the building and shaping of a new form of opera, and there was no way of doing this without a violent attack by every weapon of literary polemics upon the prevailing tradition. Fundamentally the attack was directed not so much against the arbitrary caprice of singers, with all its destructive effect on the sense of the drama, nor even against the convention of the male soprano. It is true that Gluck dispenses with coloratura, but he makes the severest demands of the Italian school on his singers; Orpheus is, after all, essentially a castrato role. The attack was aimed rather at the opera libretto of his time, which had reached its most beguiling literary form in Metastasio's much lauded dramas, set to music hundreds of times—and even by the young Gluck himself. The opera of intrigue, clad in historical or classical garb, was now to give place to the tragic conflicts of all time. The story was to return to its simplest form. Instead of the conventions of the aria-opera—the most enervating feature of which was the "metaphor aria," introduced solely to provide the composer with a suggestion for a picturesque accompaniment—the musician was to acknowledge the supremacy of the dramatist. Standardized sentiment, polite "delicacy," the avoidance of all vivid expression, the bloodless idealization of the characters—all this was to give way to living figures. The traditional plot, in the case of Metastasio chiefly concerned with love and tragically helpless heroism, was to yield to genuine passions.

Gluck's greatness lies not in the fact that he made these demands, but in the way in which as an artist he fulfilled them, in the importance he attached to the development of the opera as a musical-dramatic entity, and in his realization, at first intellectual and then musical, of the essential characters of his personages. Orpheus, the bard and fond young husband; Alcestis, the self-sacrificing wife; the effeminate Phrygian Paris, contrasted with Helen, the vigorous Spartan; the warlike Achilles; Agamemnon distraught by his terrible dilemma as father and king; the sorceress Armida; Iphigenia, priestess and sister; Thoas, the grim and superstitious barbarian—Gluck saw into the nature of them all and portrayed them with elemental rhythms, virile austerity, and a minimum of purely "musical" music, straining his untiring energies in the attainment of subtle dramatic interpretation. Strong in purpose, in Vienna and in Paris alike he pursued his ideal. How far above the cheap plaster-antiques of his age stand his vivid conceptions and visions of these classic characters! How grand the scenes that Gluck succeeded for the first time in welding into

a whole from solo, dance, and chorus! What an art was his in accumulation, contrast, and peroration! He had the power of creating an inner unity that replaced the unity of conventional form. In *Orfeo*, for the first time in the history of opera, Gluck employs accompanied recitative throughout in place of secco recitative. The chorus of mourners, interrupted by Orpheus' lamentations, his descent to Hades, the chorus and dance of the Furies, appeased by his playing until, terrible still, they lay themselves to rest; then the change from this scene to the Elysian Fields, where the orchestra magically evokes Nature translated to the heavenly sphere and the choral round of the souls of the blest; then again the scenes of mourning in *Alceste*, among the noblest in all opera; the excited choruses of the people in *Iphigénie en Aulide*, the Scythian choruses and dances in *Iphigénie en Tauride*, the scenes of Orestes' madness—what inspiration, what poetry, what dramatic intensity are here! Note, too, how Gluck in the overture to the first *Iphigénie* discloses the forces and passions governing the play which are later to be worked out in the drama, thus creating the perfect example of the opera prelude. His triumph was inevitable. To deal the collapsing Metastasian Renaissance opera a mortal blow was easy; but Gluck by his reforms overthrew the French conventional heroic opera as well. True, his imitators inherited little more than the soulless shell of his creations. The great choral scenes, the ballets, the declamatory pathos became more and more shallow in the opera of the First Republic, and in the work of the last of his direct followers, GASPARO SPONTINI—who nevertheless felt a breath of his genius—led to the empty monstrosities of the Empire period. Gluck never had a true successor.

Modern Instrumental Music—Haydn

At the same time that Gluck was writing the works
that were to reform opera, and opera buffa was
creating its own individual style, while the French
opéra comique and the German Singspiel were just
beginning their history and offering song a definite
refuge in which to try out its wings, instrumental
music underwent a change of style which may be
summed up as emancipation from the tyranny of the
basso continuo and the formation of a new conception
of the nature of the sonata.

In the course of its development the figured bass
had not only been a method of performance which
had brought into complete subjection every form of
concerted music, solo clavier music alone escaping; it
was also in itself a compendium of the fundamental
rules of composition, offering a practical understanding of the functions of sound and instruction in correct part-writing. It was by studying thorough-bass
that Bach's composition pupils learned their harmony.
As appreciation spread of the theory of harmonic
principles on the lines first laid down by Rameau,
the continuo sank slowly into oblivion. A new kind of
melody, a new style of composition arose—not in the
solo cantata or solo sonata, which clung longest to
the continuo, but in the trio and the quartet. The
idea of the continuo necessarily implied a number of
voices which were not written out but were left to
the player and depended entirely on the degree of his

skill. From now on, each voice had not only to play its part in the harmony but also to maintain a melodic line; both claims had to be fulfilled. The whole texture gained both in freedom and in inevitability, and the play of the voices—now one springing into prominence, now another—took on an altogether new significance. The "dramatic" sonata had come into being.

Its nature was new, the laws it obeyed as far removed as possible from those of the fugue; for while in the fugue the first condition is that the theme itself has to be something, the various motives which together make up the theme of the sonata mean in themselves very little—the interest lies in what becomes of them. While the fugue flows smoothly—its form conditioned by the accumulation or reduction of the voices, its climaxes achieved through melodic-contrapuntal concentration—the sonata is homophonic; the theme it presents is a whole containing its own contrasting elements—separate motives that can be split up—and strict part-writing no longer plays the smallest part. The factor of contrast is most forcibly developed in the dualism of the first and second themes in the first movement of the sonata—a dualism that has to be resolved in the course of the piece. The first theme may be, for instance, energetic and manly, the second melodious and womanly, and we must be convinced by the end of the movement that the pair have been well and truly mated. The whole cyclic form of the sonata, indeed, depends upon the unification of starkly opposite elements.

The first movement was the backbone of the new sonata form. Here a fresh significance was gained for the return of the principal theme by force of the dramatic conflict that had gone before. The second movement, slow and song-like, was given to a quiet expression of emotion; variation form was here often

adopted. The third, the minuet, was a practically
unaltered survival from the suite and so represented
the tradition of popular art. An independent, contrasting trio was inserted before the repetition. In the
concluding movement, the finale, the sonata came to
be rounded off generally by the rondo. This had
once been a "galant" piece much favoured by the
French cembalists, who attached principal importance
to its episodical "divertissements," which merely alternated with the rondo theme. But in the sonata the
interest of rondo form shifted to an artful hide-and-
seek—to the dismissal of the theme and to witty, unexpected ways of reintroducing it. As in the minuet,
here again, to wind up the sonata, a hearty folk-spirit
prevails, balancing the intellectuality of the first movement; for this was the nature and function of the new
sonata, to compose premeditated and unpremeditated
art—the life of the mind and that of simple being, the
problematic and the instinctive, and individual and
communal feeling—into a hitherto undreamt-of harmony.

It cannot be said with certainty where the modern instrumental style originated. What is certain is
that the fluent melodiousness of opera buffa quickly
made its mark on instrumental composition. PERGO-
LESI, the composer of *La Serva Padrona*, also wrote
trio sonatas full of a new spirit and an invention
stimulated by operatic melody; and we must not
forget Gluck, who was a pupil of GIOVANNI BATTISTA
SAMMARTINI, the Milanese composer of operas and
symphonies. Just as in Pergolesi's music Neapolitan
local colour was characteristically used for the first
time, so in the South German, Austrian, and Bohemian
representatives of the new instrumental music there
sprang a fresh source of unsophisticated melodic
invention. In his indifference to conventional limits

of expression, in the range of feeling in his music and its sudden contrasts, the Bohemian composer Johann Stamitz showed himself so fresh and vital that he may be considered the originator of the contrasted sonata allegro and the intimate slow movement. In 1742 Stamitz came to Mannheim; from this centre his style and that of his fellow-artists and pupils spread so quickly and effectively that, from now on, the leadership in symphony and sonata was transferred to Germany. Paris—not to mention Italy, where opera was becoming the one and only object of interest—was taken completely by surprise and suddenly found itself quite out of the running with Germany. The French were still honouring in Gossec a happy imitator of Stamitz at a time when at home Stamitz had already become an almost historical figure.

Symphony and chamber music were not at first strictly separated in the new style. Works were written to do double duty, with simple scoring for chamber music and then with added wind instruments and multiplied strings to serve as symphonies. The changed attitude showed itself in the treatment of the wind. In the older style the wind instruments —flute, oboe, trumpet—had had solo parts and were used in contrast to the tutti; but now they had to take part with the rest, to play if need be at the octave, and generally to provide colour, richness, and a solid background. It was a long time before the single wood-wind instruments and, among the brass, the increasingly popular pair of horns—the trumpet, meanwhile, having deteriorated almost into an instrument of mere noise—again won their share as soloists in the symphonic scheme and were again allowed to have their own say amid the discourse of the strings.

The hall-mark of the new style, however, was its characteristic dynamics. True, musicians had long

before understood how to vitalize their melody by
dynamic means for the sake of expressiveness and
animation in performance. But with the Mannheimers a wealth of tone-gradations between extremes
of fortissimo and pianissimo and abrupt dynamic
contrasts formed an essential effect of their art, which
they exploited to the point of abuse and deliberate
disregard of the natural accent of music. This was
the "Mannheim mannerism" against which Leopold
Mozart once warned his son. The triumph of the
Mannheim orchestra was its world-famed crescendo,
executed by string band with horns. The age of the
continuo had in the concerto grosso enjoyed full
scope for its own kind of dynamic effects, which
consisted of alternations of loud and soft, each with
its definitely limited volume according to the tone of
this or that group of instruments engaged. Now, in the
new symphony, the art of dynamic transition provided
the degrees between loud and soft. The whole body of
strings proceeds with a thematic segment to rise
gradually or quickly from the faintest whisper to a
roar of sound, and the tension created culminates in
a crashing climax. A new world of emotional excitement thus entered into instrumental music, and this
new possession, this elemental means of effect, was
found to be the very thing for opera overtures, whence
its riotous spirit freely spread to the concert symphony. Neither Haydn nor Mozart made use of the
Mannheim crescendo in their far nobler and more harmonious works. There still glimmers in the dynamics
of their symphonies the example of the concerto
grosso, with its calmer alternations between the tutti
and the more gentle groups of instruments. The first
true heir of the Mannheimers was Beethoven, who
out of the tremendous tension and tumult of his soul,

first produced significance and justification for what with them had been a mere play for effect.

The South Germans, too, and especially the Viennese school, helped in the enfranchisement of music from the basso continuo with serenades and cassations written for outdoor performance. They brought into their works a fresh, clear stream of simple melody. The North Germans failed to take this step towards a popular style and consequently lost contact—until the coming of Brahms—with the march of great instrumental art, although they had produced a leader and innovator in the person of Bach's second son, Carl Philipp Emanuel. Fruitful and many-sided though his whole production was, C. P. E. BACH exerted his strongest influence through his clavier sonatas. The music presents the most luxuriant testimony of the age of sensibility. It is full of sighs, echoes, and tearful effusions, yet in the quick movements also full of surprises and unconventional, not to say coquettish, details. In this he was the pupil of the greatest Italian instrumental composer of the eighteenth century, Domenico Scarlatti, whose harpsichord sonatas, in their wit, humour and originality, remain unrivalled to this day. For Bach the clavichord was an instrument of universal significance, his sonata a vessel of endless capacity. He introduced into it elements from the concerto and the symphony and, according to his mood, alternated between formality and rhapsody. His sentimentality was a malady of that period of musical as well as literary "Sturm und Drang," which had to be resisted by the composers who were striving towards the new style. The three greatest of these, who all in their different ways owed C. P. E. Bach a debt of gratitude, raised and transfigured the affectation of emotion into emotion itself.

A parallel to the relation between C. P. E. Bach and the three supreme masters of instrumental music is presented by the tentative appearance of eighteenth-century song and the wonderful lyrical florescence witnessed, after a long winter, in the early years of the next century. A little circle of musicians in Berlin, their leading spirit an amateur, first occupied themselves with the revival of song pure and simple. Under the influence of the French chanson they set their faces against Italian formalism and flourishes and pinned their faith to simplicity and a style racy of the soil. Their aim was to return to "natural" melody; in other words, to discover the melody inherent in the text of a given poem. This meant forswearing all the principles of the aria. In point of fact, practically all they achieved was this rather negative program. Before the true Lied could come into being, there was needed first a corpus of poetry sprung from deeper and purer sources than the Anacreontic school, Hagedorn's Frenchified wit, or Gellert's pedestrianism. It was Klopstock who fired the imagination of Gluck and of Hiller's pupil Neefe, and the latter in his turn passed on Klopstock's spirit to Beethoven. Without Neefe there would have been no *Adelaïde*. The true springtime of song appeared, however, when Claudius, Herder, and the Göttingen circle of poets— Bürger, Hölty, the Stolbergs, and Goethe, the greatest of them all—brought back into German poetry the true spirit of the race. From their lyrics that intimate composer JOHANN ABRAHAM PETER SCHULZ learned once more to listen for the tune suggested by a simple stanza and to make melody out of the very spirit of the poem. His *Trost für mancherlei Tränen* and *Neujahrslied* are songs that live on to this day as examples of great riches in a little room. His successors, composers like Reichardt and Zelter in the north, Schubart and Zumsteeg in the south, began at length to mark out the territory of the German solo and choral song; they freed the ballad from the flaccidity of the cantata form and cleared a way for Schubert and Loewe.

Of the three classical masters the one who most gladly and emphatically acknowledged his obligation to C. P. E. Bach was the eldest, Joseph Haydn. To him nevertheless is due the eclipse of Bach's mere elegance and affected sentiment—one of the benefactions this great musician bestowed on art. Only in the clavier sonata, in which Haydn is not altogether at his ease, is C. P. E. Bach's influence in some measure traceable; and even here it is more technical than spiritual. In his weaker works, which include a proportion of his sacred and secular vocal compositions, Haydn may seem a "period" composer, redolent of the pigtails and powder of his century. But the proportion of inferior works is very much smaller than might be supposed from the neglect into which they have been allowed to fall; while in his quartets, symphonies, and both his oratorios he helped the "natural man" of Rousseau's philosophy to the freedom of music, and did so without sacrificing a jot of art or intellect.

Of all the great masters Haydn was the one who served the longest and most severe apprenticeship, and in this, as in everything else, he had himself alone to thank. The son of a poor wheelwright in Lower Austria, he grew up among artisans and labourers, and no one cared whether there were the making in him of more than a chorister or a street fiddler. That irresistible urge of his to make music he had to nourish upon the merest crumbs of theory, painfully picked up for himself. But his contrapuntal instinct was so strong, his vein of melody so unfailing, that his works pleased from the first and rapidly paved the way for him to the post of Kapellmeister in the household of one of the many music-loving members of the Austrian nobility. In the isolation of Eisenstadt and Estoras, where he was obliged continually to provide new music for his princely employer, and in constant intercourse with a by no means meagre orchestra, Haydn developed the original invention, the freshness and sincerity of his melodic style, and the many-sidedness of his musical form, the things that made him the sanest and most spontaneous of all the great masters.

He worked slowly and circumspectly. His first actual symphony known to us dates from his twenty-seventh year. During the next twelve years his symphonic output—even if we assume that much has been lost—barely amounts to four symphonies a year. Each one of them is a witness to earnest and independent effort and adventure. How easy it would have been for him to take over ready-made forms and any number of details of melodic, dynamic, and orchestral technique from his forerunners and contemporaries! He despised them. What prevailed with them was affectation of feeling and facile cumulations and climaxes— games played for their own sake; but with him, strength and serious purpose and a creativeness sprung from vital experience and shaped according to a secret plan. Instead of frivolous trifling he had wit and humour; instead of their toy counters his coin was the full-weighted gold of thought.

Haydn was already celebrated in Paris as a composer of symphonies and quartets and was nearing his sixties when he made the great discovery of his life—the principle of thematic development in the "working-out" section of sonata form. He had declared his principle to the world in the year 1781 in the six "Russian quartets," which he himself described as being written in "quite a new and special way."

With Haydn's predecessors, and in his own earlier works, that section of a sonata movement after the double bar and before the return of the principal subject in the tonic had seldom been more than an episode which proceeded by sequences to a modest little melodic digression and was soon home again. Haydn now made of the development section the core and focus of the sonata movement. His "new and special way" consisted in drawing out and putting to the test the forces latent in his group of themes and thus giving an altogether new meaning and value to the recapitulation and thence to the whole melodic action of the sonata. He began to invent motifs with a view to their use in the development section. Already in the exposition of the theme each part in the quartet becomes independent, thinking its own thought as it pursues the main theme in its tranference from voice to voice, and yet not deviating from the subject of the debate. Then in the development the melodic material becomes involved in positively dramatic action, engineered by the composer's superb command of a combination of strict and free style. Here was a new application of counterpoint by which instrumental music won, as it were, its "Third Empire" and infinite enrichment of its consciousness and independence.

Not that Haydn discarded the principle of strict polyphony. He had all along known how to write counter-subjects that were true melodies and, finding examples of fugal movements in works of the Vienna and Mannheim schools, he adopted these with characteristic ardour and spirit. In the symphonies of his critical decade he clearly revelled in problems of strict form—in an Adagio in double counterpoint, in an Andante worked in canon. Later on, when he was absolute lord and master and the strict style his

very obedient servant, it amused him to apply it to his
most light-hearted movements, to his minuets and the
humorous passages of his finales. So did Haydn
triumph equally over the "elegant" style of his century
and over its contemporary antithesis, the "learned"
style, which during the homophonic vogue had lost
touch with true polyphony.

Then in the decade following the "Russian quartets" he found a fresh source of incitement and instruction in the work of his greatest contemporary,
Mozart. This he assiduously studied and, without
imitating it, he built upon it new creations. His
thematic material now became simpler and at the
same time richer and sweeter. A homely songfulness
flowed into his melody, and he delighted in producing out of the simplest idioms those wonders of
multiform expression characteristic of the sonata
developments of his maturity. This last and ripest
Haydn knew better even than Mozart the secret of
giving to a whole quartet or symphony that mysterious unity which makes its four movements seem
to us like different aspects of a simple, vividly characterized being, renders every one of these works unmistakably distinct from any other, and convinces us that
each finale is the inevitable outcome of the whole
preceding musical action, forming its dénouement and
joyous consummation. He himself spoke of "moral
characters" delineated in his symphonies, and his contemporaries thoroughly appreciated this characteristic
content, which they sought to define by bestowing
special designations and nicknames on different works
and movements.

While the first movement of the sonata developed
its perfected form in Haydn's hands, the second he
deepened with emotion from a generous heart and

with hymn-like song. An immortal example is the *Emperor's Hymn*, which he made use of in a magnificent set of variations in one of the string quartets. And what a different thing is his minuet from the mincing or pompous movements, powdered and bewigged, with which his contemporaries concluded their symphonies! Here he frolics and makes merry, sets dancers' toes a-tingling, and can burst out with roaring humour; but also he can strike those notes of seriousness, indignation, and rage which lend the third movement a full symphonic weight and without which Beethoven's scherzo might never have been. His trump cards, however, he saved for his finales. The wealth of high spirits and wild-fire movement, the humour, and the vital union of law and liberty that are here represent a summit of art where Haydn stands alone. Haydn's quartet and his symphony are a supreme achievement of the human mind—a heritage which the glib epithet "Papa Haydn" has all too long caused to be underrated.

In his two oratorios, *The Creation* and *The Seasons*, the master of instrumental music was greatly influenced by the Handelian model, from which, however, the result was far removed, since in the meantime the development of symphonic writing, the relation of the accompaniment to the vocal line, the new feeling for nature—which in music had above all found utterance in orchestral commentary—and the expansion of opera and Singspiel at Mozart's hands had transformed the whole spirit of things. Between Handel's oratorios and Haydn's came all the gains of music's "storm and stress" period. Haydn conquered for himself the style of his oratorio and its sublimity, and *The Creation* thus represents a landmark in the history of the form.

Mozart

Mozart had not the time for a slow and steady development such as benefited Haydn's life-work. All that is contained of human destiny within the limits of a short life of not quite thirty-six years is indicated by that dreadful descent which leads from the pampering of the child prodigy by the courts of Europe to the begging letters of the last years in Vienna and his burial in a pauper's grave. The vital energy, lacking in Mozart for the shaping of his career, in spite of his keen eye for men and conditions, was consumed wholly in artistic "speculation"; for indeed his dæmon did everything that was required for the purpose of fulfilling his artistic mission. Mozart was the son of an excellent musician who as an instrumental composer represented the good average of his time and who recognized his child's uncanny gifts and did not, at least consciously, misuse them. The boy grew up where South German symphonic and chamber music were, so to speak, in the air. At the age of six he went to Vienna. The time between his seventh and tenth years was occupied by an ambitious artistic tour, taking in Paris and London, where the new, free clavier style of Schobert and the symphonic pliability of Carl Friedrich Abel and Johann Christian Bach, as well as the latter's facile operatic principles, were communicated to the boy. At twelve he wrote his first opera for Vienna; at thirteen, with his mind still more matured, he undertook his first journey to Italy (to be followed by two others) and took his place as a rival in the ranks of the Italian opera-composers representing the latest Neapolitan tendencies. His journey to Mannheim and Paris, which may be regarded as the last of his apprenticeship, brought him into touch with experiments in national German opera and with Gluck's operatic ideal, half accommodated to and half forced upon French tendencies.

Mozart's training was a spiritual process such as only a miraculous artistic organism could venture upon and overcome. The acquaintances with new forms of art and new individualities were the true experiences in Mozart's development, which in his boyhood still resulted in frequent acceptance of influences of all sorts, good and bad, so much so that the youthful composer's style was subject to iridescent changes from work to work; indeed, as a ripe master he continued to take delight in assuming a stylistic mask foreign to him. Before long, however, a complete sublimation and new formation of alien artistic peculiarities occurred, a continual absorption of sympathetic elements. The result was an incomparable melodic richness and taste, a musical and spiritual flexibility, a formal assurance and clarity that has not its equal. This clarifying affected not only the structure of his instrumental and operatic forms but also the inner texture of his musical idiom. Never has the natural strife between homophony and polyphony, between melody and counterpoint, been more completely settled. This most spontaneous of melodists appears to have had polyphonic expression at his command as a gift of nature, for all that its acquisition demonstrably cost him some pains in his youth.

No species of music current in his time was left untouched by Mozart, none is without a matchless

contribution from his pen; but it was his work in
the domain of opera, symphony, and chamber music
that was to be most influential. In the matter of
opera, it is true, discrimination is indicated. Most of
his "serious" operas fall into the period of his youth,
and however astonishing a maturity in vocal and
orchestral modelling they may often betray, they are
still the work of a boy and follow the unhealthy
principle of the latest—the so-called third—Neopoli-
tan school, with its sketchy treatment of recitative,
its empty pathos, and, to use a contemptuous phrase
of Gluck's, its constant "smelling of music." Then
La Clemenza di Tito, although Mozart's last operatic
creation, was a work thrown on paper in haste and
under harassing conditions, wonderful in its certainty
of style, but impossible to awaken to any dramatic
life, and in fact not altogether comparable in this
respect with many of the earlier settings of the same
text.

Mozart's most captivating opera seria, *Idomeneo*,
written by him with the most ambitious care for
Munich at the age of twenty-five and held in high
esteem in his lifetime, has been connected with the
operatic art of Gluck because of some outward
resemblances; but in spite of dramatic choruses and
ballet music, Mozart shows in this very work, with
its bewitching vocal treatment of the arias and concerted pieces and its admirable orchestral details,
that the laws of Gluck's opera had not yet dawned
upon him—this did not happen in an altogether
decisive way until he produced *Die Entführung aus
dem Serail*—and that he approached truth in musical characterization from an entirely different angle.
For Mozart, opera seria remained a piece of musical
jewellery into the set forms of which he inserted the
most precious stones, although for his largest aria

forms he preferred those which combine a preparatory slow movement with a brilliant allegro—those,
that is, which contain a development or at any rate
link up two static lyrical elements. In his best period
he produced a whole series of musical gems of this
sort, either as extra numbers for operas to which they
were foreign or as independent concert pieces. To
become a great master of the opera seria Mozart
would have required a wholly different development
and, above all, a longer life than that vouchsafed to
him.

It is otherwise with Mozart's imperishable buffo
operas and his German "Singspiele." The former
reach the height of their species, and indeed far
more than that; the latter have, next to their own
value, the profoundest historical significance. The
history and nature of both species must now be studied
more closely.

Opera buffa was, much like the early villanella,
whose fate it shared to some extent, partly the child
of a spirit of parody and of satirical humour. The
Roman opera of the seventeenth century already, and
still more the Venetian, was partial to comic servants
who derisively parodied the pathetic events preceding
their scenes. Then, at the beginning of the eighteenth
century, the opposition to the unnaturalness of opera
seria, which had so often formulated itself theoretically
and led to its transformation, found vent in the intermezzi that were wont to be inserted between the
three acts of a "serious" opera. Comedy with music,
we know, has never ceased to satirize grand opera, and
as late as the nineteenth century not only did the more
refined parts of Offenbach's operetta take sustenance
from it, but operatic criticism found its monumental
expression and its artistic idealization in Wagner's *Die
Meistersinger*.

Satire, however, did not suffice. Of the two forms
in which opera buffa appeared, the intermezzo in
two parts inclined more towards the figures of the
old Italian *commedia dell'arte:* the captain, the vil-
lainous old hag, the amorous and duped guardian
with his ward and her inevitable lover, and Pulcinella were taken over in all their forms. The most
famous and still living example of these intermezzi
is Pergolesi's *Serva Padrona.* At the same time, and
clearly in Venice quite as early as in Naples, the
fully developed opera buffa in three acts took the
stage; in Naples rather with popular types with
the text sung in dialect, while Venice before long supplied one of the most fertile of librettists, Carlo Goldoni,
who began early to transfer his characters and his
half-droll, half-sentimental mixture of styles to the
opera buffa, since when it has followed all the small
deviations of literary comedy without sacrificing
anything of its earlier contents. Thus we find in the
second half of the century a variegated mixing and
juxtaposition of the elements of classical comedy with
its guiding motives of disguise, mistaken indentity,
and recovery, its political and artistic satire, its sentimental family histories, its Offenbachiads, its fantastic displays of magic and fairy-tales, its ancient
comedy of masquerade.

No wonder that opera buffa was not long in taking
precedence over opera seria. While dramatically it
was devised to bring wit, surprise, and lively change
into play, it also had a musical advantage over "serious"
opera, which had degenerated into a bundle of arias,
in its steadily increasing wealth of forms. The intermezzo already, though short of characters, shows the
piquant dramatic duet and trio; but the developed
buffo opera soon gains introductions and finales in
addition to these: the former an incomparable means

of exposition, introducing with musical incisiveness several persons at once in some characteristic situation, the latter tying and confusing the dramatic knot with the utmost vivacity for the benefit of eye and ear. This was opera's third triumph over the spoken drama, although the beginnings of the simultaneous characterization of the personages in buffo opera had long been prepared in other fields. The first triumph was due to song itself, which in an artistic sense is truer than mere speech; the second to the revelation of inarticulate secrets by means of orchestral expression; the last to the possibility of representing a scene at one and the same time with a heightened vitality or, if you like, with the utmost truth to nature, and with the greatest ideal precision.

Not all buffo-composers found this full and ripe form of the dramatic finale convenient. In the work of NICCOLO PICCINNI himself (Gluck's Paris rival), the most amiable musician among them, we find next to it a mere chain of arias, cavatinas, and duets. But this dramatic finale, the prettiest examples of which were furnished by Guglielmi and Paisiello among the Italians, led—as a reward of enterprise—to a new conquest: the unification of the scene by means of the summarizing orchestral motif—at that time, of course, always entrusted to the string instruments. Thence the step to the abolition of the stylized aria, to the opera composed right through, was, or should have been, by no means a long one. Instead of that, opera buffa at an early stage borrowed, in addition to its own forms, those of opera seria, and what it thus gained in musical wealth it lost, one must confess, in purity of style. A taste for fantastic subjects, and an admixture of the sentimental family play demanded a pair of languishing lovers who were expected to offer the public the grand aria with its coloratura ornamentation. Opera buffa had begun by scoffing at opera seria; by adopting the da-capo aria the victim in turn enjoyed its most subtle triumph. By 1740 already we meet in Venetian programs with a separation of the characters into *parti buffe* and *parti serie*, into comic and serious parts, and Mozart's *Don Giovanni*, with Don Ottavio, Donna Anna, the Commandant, and Elvira on the one side and Leporello, Zerlina, and Masetto on the other, historically belongs decidedly to this category.

Needless to say, Mozart transforms what his precursors contented themselves with making into a conventional mixture of styles to please a public that demanded all the pleasures of opera, tranforms it merely by his touch into an artistically truthful mirror of human destiny, where scurrility and mirth are reflected side by side with tragedy and supernatural gloom; or else he elevates it into the supersensual and therefore reconciling light of an immortal serenity and grace. In his last three buffo operas, *Le Nozze di Figaro*, *Don Giovanni*, and *Così fan tutte*, for which fortune sent him a clever librettist in the Venetian Jew Lorenzo da Ponte and, in two of them at least, true comedy with living figures and an indestructibly vital heritage of the world's literature, Mozart accepted all the forms of the Italians, but recast them in the cleansing fire of his unique musicality. The most worn melodic coin becomes pure gold again, mere formality is transformed into spirit and meaning. Above all, as a token of tense dramatic life, there is his orchestra—"A mighty number of notes," observed an exalted contemporary; "Just as many as are required," retorted Mozart—which illuminates the most delicate psychological reactions with unsuspected resourcefulness and refinement, and with its richness and beauty of treatment of the wind instruments marks a new departure.

But the incomparable quality of Mozart's operas lies in the miraculous harmony of the profoundest dramatic truth and characterization (which has given us the imperishable personages of *Figaro* as well as the iridescent picture of the universe and the moral decision of *Don Giovanni*) with perfect musical form. In the musico-dramatic construction of the first act of *Figaro*, in its sparkling first finale, which paints a dramatic and psychological action of the utmost complexity with the greatest truth, depth, and clearness, in that tremendous opening of *Don Giovanni*, that point of equilibrium is attained at which the seeming incompatibles of conflicting operatic exigencies appear for once to be reconciled. How enigmatically simple and just is the characterization of the arias! How naturally truthful and yet idealized is, for example, the sweet confusion of the adolescent's longing for love in the few bars which make up Cherubino's aria and canzone! How each figure in the concerted pieces, from the foremost to the least, the apparently most subsidiary, from the Count to Don Curzio, from Elvira to Masetto, speaks its own language! How consummately clear and bright, and yet so sweet and saturated, is the melodic idiom in *Figaro;* to what half-shadows and burning lights is it intensified in *Don Giovanni;* how subtly is coloratura used as ironical exaggeration in *Così fan tutte;* what a novel employment Mozart still finds for it as a naïve symbol for blind feminine rage in *Die Zauberflöte!* How perfectly do the overtures paint partly the substance of the drama and partly—as in *Don Giovanni*—the opposition of tragic forces!

Mozart's German operas—*Die Entführung aus dem*

Serail and *Die Zauberflöte*—have a comparatively
short pedigree, which this time points to Paris and
London. In Paris, too, the high-stilted grand opera
was a welcome butt for ridicule and parody, both
for the priviliged stage of the "Italiens" and for the
later theatres at the fairs, where Harlequin took all
operatic topics as occasions for his satire. In the
same way a national protest against the importation
of Italian opera assumed a parodistic and much imitated form in London in *The Beggar's Opera* (1728).
Music's share in such works was originally restricted
to modest interpolations of songs; but it grew when
in 1752 a company of Italian buffo singers introduced
two intermezzi by Pergolesi to the Parisians, thus
unchaining a violent conflict of opinions concerning
the relative merits of buffo opera and national musical
plays—a conflict which induced French composers to
undertake a musical elaboration of their opéra comique.
Duni, Philidor, Monsigny, and Grétry were its most
gracious exponents and led it near the beginnings of
romantic opera. That the old "vaudeville" comedy,
too, was capable of accommodating a greater musical richness Gluck proved with the most developed
and influential of his comic operas—which also had
an influence on Mozart's *Die Entführung*—*La Ren-
contre imprévue*, itself, it is true, strongly affected
by Italian suggestions.

While comic opera reached Vienna in French
guise, companies of German actors began by taking
possession of two downright English pieces from the
succession of *The Beggar's Opera*. A new turn was
very soon taken by the Singspiel, however, when it
came into the hands of the librettist Christian Felix
Weisse, who was familiar from personal observation with the opéra comique, and of the amiable,
cultivated, and somewhat philistine Johann Adam

Hiller in Leipzig. The contrast between town and country, between pure nature according to the conception of Rousseau and the corruption of the upper classes, was Hiller's favourite subject and gave him the excuse to cultivate a folksong-like melody, a simple form of song, without compelling him to renounce the treasures of an Italianate type of aria. Here, too, a blend of styles was accomplished when Mozart, along with other Viennese masters, took a hand with his freshly youthful *Entführung* in what was now "German opera," which apart from the connecting recitative, now replaced by spoken dialogue, coveted all the fruits of both buffo and serious opera. What again distinguishes Mozart here is his warmth and delicacy as well as the sharpness and fullness of his musical character-drawing. What a magnificent figure is that atrabilious pot-belly of an Osmin!

But to all this something new and unexpected is added in *Die Zauberflöte*. Here the Masonic symbolism, which the librettist Schikaneder worked into his crude but effective play of magic and machinery, fired Mozart's imagination to the creation of the secular solemnity of that prevalent tone which manifests itself in Sarastro's tranquil strains, the grand choruses of the priests, the airy trios of the three Genii, and the hymn-fantasy of the Armed Men. The transfiguring power of this music overcomes the trite rationalism of the play's meaning and language, rendering its incidents truly symbolic. The whole of German romantic opera took its departure from its wondrous tone. With this one work Mozart gained for German opera a position equal to that held by the idealistic drama of Schiller and Goethe. In much the same way, with a single song that does not exhibit Lied form as we now understand it—his setting of Goethe's *Veilchen*—he indicated a new and adventurous path to the whole nineteenth century.

As an instrumental composer Mozart is scarcely less great and important; it must even be said that he was originally and essentially an instrumental composer. Much as he did to extend the work of his forerunners, especially that of Haydn, he yet impressed the stamp of his own mind on every form and species, from the clavier piece in variation form to the symphony. With the development of sonata form he concerned himself less than one might have supposed. His especial affection went to the concerto, in which festivity and dramatic spirit, strength and grace are expressed in the most polished and ingenious manner by the distribution of thesis and antithesis and where, following the model of the "London" Bach, he treated the second subject—and therefore sonata form—seriously. Although himself a keyboard-player, he did not care for a virtuoso's treatment of the clavier sonata, which he cannot be said to have greatly favoured. He much preferred to associate the pianoforte with chamber music and to use it for the richest combinations with string and wind instruments in order to throw a keener light on his wonderful melodies; witness his Quintet for Pianoforte and Wind Instruments, his piano quartets, or his Trio for Pianoforte, Clarinet, and Viola. But Mozart occupies also one of the highest positions as a master of the string trio (although with a single example), the string quartet, and even more, perhaps, the string quintet, much as, here again, he owed to Haydn's example. It is indeed a long way from the earlier instrumental works, with their Italian parading of chords, their rushing passages, their sweet melodic contrasts, to the six quartets dedicated to Haydn, with their wholly German character, in which *Magic*

Flute sounds are to be heard already and where Mozart's abundance of melodic force, of form, of artistry is displayed with endless resource.

His last and most perfect gifts to orchestral music we possess are the three symphonies dating from the summer of 1788, which embrace such wide contrasts: the E flat, the most Haydnish in form and content, the G minor, luxuriating in dejected resignation, and the C major, music that rouses itself to luminous, serene, and manly strength. What is foreshadowed in Haydn's symphonic themes, songfulness in the allegro movements, becomes plainly discernible in Mozart. What distinguishes him from Haydn —who after Mozart's death continued to develop the symphonic form still more widely and consciously —is a greater wealth of half-shades and transitions, a sensitiveness to sound that has remained altogether unique and was never again to be attained, and above all an entirely different sphere of emotion, at once sensuous and non-sensuous, hovering between grace and melancholy, indeed often changing colour with a lightning-like abruptness. Mozart draws from a deeper well than the more earthly Haydn, a well at the bottom of which romantic lights begin to gleam. For that Mozartian "serenity" is altogether a very strange thing. Not to mention the famous works in minor keys, only those who know certain major movements of his, such as the finale of the A major Quartet or the wild, disconsolate mirth of the Quintet in D, written a year before his death, and have rightly understood the dæmonic fatalism with which they glow, will see the true significance of the clarity and joyousness Mozart could set off on such a dark background. For them the magical, athematic melodies, which are a characteristic of the later Mozartian rondo form and seem to bid the wheel of inexorable destiny

stand still for once, will become a joy that will never
fade.

Beethoven

Close though Beethoven stands in time to the two
musicians whose pupil he was and with whom he
forms what is commonly thought of as the classical
triad, his name is in itself enough to suggest a new
world of music. Beethoven's whole position in regard to life and art was different from that of his
predecessors. Haydn had to submit almost all his life
to the old conditions of a musical retainer; Mozart
broke free from the feudal order of things only to
come to grief economically. Beethoven by force of
character and passionate integrity stood face to face
with the world, a free man. What he demanded of
society was the wherewithal to work unhindered,
and he demanded it as a right, knowing how much he
had to give in return. He had the Revolution behind
him. The great artist was rooted in a great man; nor
can it ever be otherwise. Goethe, rightly in a way,
called him "an utterly untamed creature," a judgment which he apparently never modified. But the
contrary is really true. Formidable though the natural forces in this man were, his moral strength was
yet greater. He, the son of a drunken court-musician
and a cook, developed the intellect to apprehend
not only the highest and subtlest problems of his
age—the age of Kant, Schiller, Goethe—but, what
is more, intuitively to master them. He never troubled

much about conventional orthography, but in his notes and letters occur flashes of intense perception and laconic phrases perfect in expression. One such is the motto of the Pastoral Symphony: "Expression of feeling rather than painting"—a phrase that settles the question of the validity of program music once and for all.

The most terrible fate that can befall a musician —deafness—drove him at the age of thirty-two to the verge of despair and suicide, but he knew he had not the right to leave the world before he had brought forth all those things of which he felt himself capable. Mistrust—worst of all the psychological afflictions of the deaf—ruined his relations with his fellow-men and resulted in conduct in regard to money matters which to this day has left a certain opening for disapprobation. The ageing Beethoven took on himself the upbringing of an undutiful nephew and thereby learned to know what pangs may afflict a father's heart. Throughout these trials he was sustained by his moral sense and his unconquerable faitn in God's goodness. Just how far the dark currents of his life influenced his music is a question not to be gone into here; but how the tumultuous natural forces of the man were brought into subjection under the empire of his mighty will, were tamed and made the servants of form and order—therein lies the unique supremacy of Beethoven the artist.

He was as rich in innate musical talent as any of the masters who have been acclaimed as infant prodigies, but his destiny was a development of peculiar arduousness as artist and as man, and he was almost twenty-five before his Op. 1, three pianoforte trios, was published. But this Op. 1 was one in which the nature of the man was declared in all its originality. From the very beginning the urge and tension in him were greater and mightier than in his predecessors. He explores new depths of the emotions; sorrow and passion are matter in his hands, and the shapes he gives them are his triumphs. Sonata form seems to have been awaiting his coming; it was now to grow to grand, to titanic proportions, and to be filled with an intenser life than ever before. Variation form is above all for Beethoven a school of energetic concentration. Again and again he is drawn to it, building on the narrowest foundations structures of the utmost diversity and imaginativeness and bending to the service of his giant will a form that had since Bach's time become frivolous and the toy of executants. How and why his groups of themes strain with so fierce a tension, the reason for the huge expansion of his developments, for the changes he introduces into the recapitulation, the new role he allots to the coda, the diversity with which he organizes the cyclic form, and the significant relationship of the different movements—all this is not to be explained on merely formal grounds. Beethoven's music is poetry. There was something he had to say, the ineffable had to be uttered. The musician, the artist in him, was servant to the prophet.

Critics have divided Beethoven's work into three periods, and between "middle" and "late" Beethoven there certainly came a lull in his productiveness which also marks a certain change of style. But from the very first his treatment of the matter of music had been poetic and imaginative. The works of the first period speak of the young master's delight in his own strength and of a bold, challenging spirit. Beethoven enjoyed taking up another's theme and showing what could be made of it. Haydn and Clementi, in particular, and Mozart too, were drawn upon for this purpose. But many a movement, many a whole sonata—thus, the Trio in C minor, some of the pianoforte sonatas, especially that in D minor, Op. 31, No. 2, the first of the string quartets, Op. 18, and the Second Symphony—point to the full-grown master of the "Eroica," a work which, as a whole, but particularly its first movement, Beethoven himself was never to surpass; in which purity of form and depth of poetic intention are perfectly matched; in which an invention, a shaping of themes, an art of preparation and transition, all of incomparable power and penetration, are only symbols of an interior conception, and this not a mere brutal battle, but the very ethos of heroism.

To the prolific period following the "Eroica" belong works in which Beethoven was powerfully preoccupied with pathos and its sublimation—the struggle with Fate and final triumph of the C minor Symphony; the sense of the blessedness of Nature's peace and of divine immanence in the "Pastoral"; the "Appassionata" Sonata; the profound Op. 59 quartets (especially the first, one of the crowns of his whole life's work). Or else the solution is sought in dithyrambic jubilation, as in the Seventh Symphony. There are also compositions that spring from almost pure founts of strength, joy, and self-dedication, such as the Fourth and Eighth symphonies, the last two pianoforte concertos, and the violin concerto.

Mere tunefulness meant, throughout his work, nothing to him. He needed it, but it was to be fought for, not an obvious thing to be accepted. It became, indeed, actually suspect to him, in the conflicts of his symphonic dramas. The whole nature of his work is bound up with the intellectuality of his art. He laboured hard, not because of any meagreness in the flow of music in him, but because he had to realize to the full the ideal of his vision. He wrestled with a theme in its constituent motifs, he

rejected and recast, refined melody and rhythm,
until the complete and perfect impression was coined.
He laboured at building and transplanting, at connexions and path-making; and at length the form
answered to the thought. When Beethoven did not
quite attain his ends he produced works, such as the
Choral Fantasia, which are like buildings with girders
still showing through the masonry. A fanciful idea
was in itself nothing to him; the greatest daring in
modulation or rhythm—and he was the greatest
master of rhythm of all the musicians—was only a
means to deepen and intensify a spiritual whole.

Entire freedom was his, however, only in instrumental music. After his cantata-like *Adelaïde* he
toiled hard at song-writing, achieving mastery at
length in his *Liederkreis*. But his only opera plainly
shows how uncongenial the great man found the
historic opera forms. *Fidelio* is a work that stands
by itself, but historically it belongs to the category
of French opéra comique in the full-grown form
represented by the operas of heroism and liberation
of the time of the Revolution. Since Pergolesi's intermezzi had excited national ambitions for opera
in Paris, "comic opera" had sturdily developed, most
notably in the works of the high-minded and pas-
sionately sincere Cherubini; it had gleaned something,
too, from Haydn's and Mozart's music. While slighter
in musical content than Italian opera buffa (it made
shift with spoken dialogue in place of recitative), it
was distinguished by a more tasteful choice of subjects
and a subtler delineation of character. Instead of the
rough humour of the Italians, it inclined to pathos;
the action was free to take a serious turn, and strong
and affecting situations were acceptable. It could, in
fact, deal with matters denied to "grand opera"; its
scope was wider, embracing as it did every stage

from idyll to tragedy, from the playful to the sublime.
Now, the heart of the matter of *Fidelio* is powerfully
affecting—the heroic deed of a devoted wife who
wrests her husband from his persecutor. For the sake
of the chorus of prisoners, the dungeon scene, and the
tremendous tumult of emotion in the duet following
Florestan's liberation Beethoven took on the work,
incidentally burdening himself with various minor
characters (Rocco, Marcelline, Jaquino, Pizzarro) and
musical numbers which were vehicles all too petty
for his purpose. That purpose was realized, in all the
splendour of unhampered inspiration, in the *Leonore*
overtures, which with his other overtures—*Coriolan*
and *Egmont*—inaugurated a new era of poetic music.
The most daring and portentous of the *Leonore* overtures is not the third, but the second.

Creation in the service of an idea becomes fully
manifest in those three groups of works which are
associated by the media employed as by the sense
of the music: in one category the Mass in D and the
Ninth Symphony, in another the last five pianoforte
sonatas, and in the third the last five quartets with
the *Grosse Fuge*. In the Mass Beethoven makes use
of the traditional liturgical text for the purpose of a
tremendous and intensely subjective disputation between man and God. In its style, in its freedom and
recklessness of expression and means the Ninth Symphony forms an antithesis to the Mass and a complement. From awe, entreaty, and unquestioning faith
the Mass proceeds to perturbation and unrest. The
symphony throws a bridge over abysses of despair,
distraction, and fond yearnings to the goal of mankind
reconciled in brotherly love and certainty of God's
fatherly goodness. There comes a point in the Mass,
in the *Agnus Dei*, at which the burden of the message
devolves upon pure instrumental music; while in the

symphony, out of the orchestral complex, human voices emerge at last, as the final and most explicit utterance of the composer's purpose. The text of the Mass is for Beethoven a means to an end, just as is his high-handed adaptation of Schiller's Ode.

In the last sonatas and quartets Beethoven's language has undergone a change. The five pianoforte sonatas form a spiritual whole. Form and syntax have an appearance of unrestricted freedom; but to look deeper is to perceive the inevitability of the organization and the relation to the whole of every part. What takes place in this fluctuating and heaving world of sound proceeds in the higher regions of excitations, as it had done in Beethoven himself; and the last quartets speak, if possible, a still more spiritual language. Gone is the pathos of the earlier works; it lies far behind us. Once only, in the heart-piercing Cavatina of the B flat Quartet, it returns with multiplied force. Elsewhere when it attempts to put in an appearance, as in the "*schwergefasste Entschluss*," "the difficult resolve," of the last quartet, smiling irony makes mock of it.

In these sublime soliloquies of a lonely soul, ranging immeasurably beyond the confines of his age, the subject-matter tends to become simpler and more aphoristic, but the treatment and articulation ever subtler. In fugato, in his "*tantôt libre, tantôt recherchée*" fugue, Beethoven seeks to master a new means of utterance at once more intense and less passionate; and variation form moves to the heights of mystical experience. There is no knowing what Beethoven had in mind to give us after these works—he died full of plans for new creations. For us they represent in energy of form and spirituality of content the supremest height to which music has attained.

The Romantic Age

When Beethoven died, in 1827, music already found itself in the midst of an intellectual movement that decided the art of the whole of the nineteenth century and to some extent that of our own days: the romantic movement. The idea of romanticism embraces such an enormous variety of elements, intellectual and emotional, that it is useless to attempt to reduce it to any simple formula. How otherwise could musicians of such various character and conflicting aims as Weber and Schubert, Schumann and Wagner, Mendelssohn and Berlioz, Brahms, Liszt, and Bruckner be enrolled under the same banner? Each of these musicians possessed certain romantic characteristics all his own, while he was at the same time linked in other ways to one or another of his fellows. The essence of romanticism lies in the incessant absorption of fresh material from musical or outside sources and the moulding of all this into new unities.

There had been romanticism in music long before there were romantic composers—long, even, before the word "romantic," a literary term to begin with, was coined. The extravagant chromaticism, suggesting a world of subtle emotions, of the last masters of the madrigal; the unfettered flight of Buxtehude's organ fantasias; the passionate poetry in Bach's expression of his longing for death; the chiaroscuro of Mozart's harmonies—all these were foreshadowings of the romantic age. What now happened was not so much a discovery as the choice of a new angle of vision. The spirit of the age regarded the things of art exclusively in a romantic light and saw in them all only the dazzling enchantment of sympathetic colours.

Thus almost the whole of Beethoven came to be hailed as romantic. The prodigious power of his symphonic works seemed a fulfilment of the oracular saying of the eighteenth-century poet Wackenroder to the effect that instrumental music was the one true art, a heaven that was to be gained by the renunciation of reality. That was one aspect; but there was another. This generation, hearing once more the strains of old German folk-poetry in *Des Knaben Wunderhorn*, found them irresistible, went back to the land, and invigorated its songs at the sources it discovered in the feelings of common folk. Occupational and social singing gave rise to a new popular song; it was the age of choral singing for the people. Great masters of romanticism, such as Mendelssohn and Schumann, and many lesser men, chief of them FRIEDRICH SILCHER, felt urged to contribute to it. The years that saw the national revival of Germany saw too the coming-of-age of the German male-voice part-song—that manifestation of a longing for national unity and the advancement of the race. Carl Maria von Weber achieved the most accomplished and ardent expression of the patriotic enthusiasm that swept Germany during the "War of Liberation"; his songs with pianoforte, too, are stamped, none more clearly, with certain essentially German features. Since then the musical health of the people has been measurable by the fluctuations in the depth and purity of the song in popular use, upon which the musical future of a people depends. Mystical seclusion, subjectivity, withdrawal from the world on the one hand,

and on the other the endeavour to place music upon a wider, popular, national basis—both tendencies belong to the contradictory characteristics of the romantic age in music.

Franz Schubert is the romantic classic, the classical romantic. He is a classic inasmuch as he learned from Mozart and still more from Beethoven, his master of masters, and entered into the inheritance of the classical forms with the genius that made him the rightful reversioner. What distinguishes him from the classic is his mastery in a hitherto unimagined realm, the magical sphere of sheer sound. Here, in the world of pure sound in which they live and move, is the ground common to all the true romantics; here is the bond that links them, the clue to their obscure relationships. Schubert led a middle-class life in a quiet unpretentious circle. The tragedy of his terribly brief career was that life and the world denied him the activities that might have brought him to full consciousness of his powers; but the smug Vienna of his time was anything but the place for that. So it is that Schubert the instrumental composer lacks Beethoven's virile, masterful power. Instead of motifs that actively work to build up subjects and make possible the drama of coherent development sections, he is content with rounded, self-contained melodies and often with amiable episodes that are mere interpolations, leading nowhere but whence they came. His sonata form can often be found fault with for excessive expansion and mere melodiousness, for lack of concentration and all that Schumann, Schubert's rediscoverer and worshipper, called "heavenly lengths." Often, but not always. Not even Beethoven himself achieved anything more striking or more terse than the volcanic climax of the first movement of the Symphony in B minor. For that matter, Schubert's apparent failings are only the reverse side of his immortal greatness. His thoughts seem to spring from the primal fount of sound and melody. While in his dances, waltzes and *Ländler*, his écossaises and marches, Schubert the folk-singer pours out the soul of the Lower Austrian homeland, the great Schubert strikes his lyre as the greatest of all nature-musicians and pantheists. To this great Schubert belong the Symphony in B minor, that incomparable song of sorrow which we wrong by calling it "Unfinished"; the great C major, with its tremendous trombone calls in the first movement, a symphony that declares Schubert to be Beethoven's peer; the String Quintet in C, the quartets in A minor and D minor; the Octet; some of the pianoforte sonatas. In other works, such as the pianoforte trios and the "Trout" Quintet, he inclines to embrace the lighter tones of easy-going Viennese virtuosity. But always he is the inexhaustible melodist, rich beyond reckoning in feeling and fancy, in tone and colour, in the art of his magical veerings between major and minor, and in the discovery by his modulations of depths of the soul never plumbed before.

Schubert's songs, however, are his peculiar glory. Here is the vital centre of his creative work. Who would understand his instrumental music must first know Schubert the lyricist. In the use he made of themes from his own songs (rarely from another's) for the variations which not seldom take the place of a slow movement in his sonatas is to be seen an obvious connexion, but there are others, and deeper ones by far.

Schubert composed many accompanied and unaccompanied part-songs for male and mixed voices, in which there is music of wonderful quality; but his real mission was to be master of the song for solo voice and pianoforte, the German song, the Lied, which is so much his creation and Germany's possession that other nations have hardly or not at all an equivalent even for the name. It is all his own, and is at the same time remarkably related to folk-song. So are wild rose and garden rose akin. Such a piece as *Der Lindenbaum* from his greater song-cycle might well return to the hedgerow and become a folk-song again.

He began as a boy of fourteen with imitations of the Swabian ballad-composer Johann Rudolf Zum-steeg, setting to music Schiller's exuberant and vivid poems, Matthison, Ossian, and much else of the sort that excited his superabundant, pictorial-musical imag-ination. This mine yielded both declamatory dross and melody of pure gold. But incredibly soon Schu-bert found the song form that was his own. It was his already on the day—October 10, 1814—when for the first time he took fire from Goethe's supreme lyric art and wrote that "lyrical monody," as it has been well called, *Gretchen am Spinnrad*, his first master-song. This form, the outcome of the relation-ship between his music and the text, is, to use a figure of speech, not a vessel of gold made to hold a precious content; rather is it to be considered as a line defining a living body. While Beethoven is cramped by a text, it is for Schubert at once an inspiration and a liberation. He can touch profundity in the simplest of strophic songs—take the setting of Goethe's *Jäger's Abendlied* for example. Indeed, only by compulsion, as it were, and for the most urgent reasons, does his song abandon strophic form; but then, with the utmost sensitiveness and a kind of clairvoyant certainty, he finds for the freest flights of his poets the appropriate flowing setting, compact of musical elements. The supreme wonder of his song is the equipoise between imagery and emotion. There is not one in which the mere descriptiveness that reduces the poetry to a bare statement prevails; his pictorialism is always suffused with feeling; his song looks both outwards and inwards, is at once subjective and objective. Between the vocal line and the accompaniment the relationship is never hard and fast, but is one of sensitive flexibility, though the voice is the predominant partner. His simplest types of accompaniment are eloquent, and so it is that he can plumb the depths with quiet utterance and rise to climaxes of supreme boldness and diversity. What wealth is his in the range of his accompaniment-figures alone; what can he not express with the least of modifications! The most splendid of his resources is harmonic —his modulation. The *"weite, hohe, herrliche Blick"* in *An Schwager Kronos*, the sunset in *Heimweh*, the lover's tears in Platen's *Du liebst mich nicht*, and a thousand other audacious strokes of genius—what a wealth is here of vivid images and at the same time of the vibrations of the soul of man! To think of the miracle of human genius is to think of Schubert. From him nothing is hidden; nothing to him was alien, nothing too lofty, from the plainest of folk-ditties to Schiller's philosophic lyricism, from the clear air of Goethe's exquisite and joyous love-poems to Novalis's mysticism—it is a world as full of emotion as of significant shapes born of an imagination not less rich nor less creative than Bach's own, a mirror and a record of his sensibility in all its delicacy, truth, and power. Most mature and most deeply affecting are the works composed towards the end of his short life: *Die schöne Müllerin* and *Die Winterreise*, both settings of verses by Wilhelm Müller, and each a veritable tragedy in the form of a succession of brief lyrics. He exhausted the realm of the Lied; all that the nineteenth century could do after him was to apply to song-writing some of the new refinements of musical style. Schubert has been unsurpassed to this day.

He occupied himself seldom, and then not very characteristically, with a form of poetry that is rooted more strongly in the popular feeling of the northern nations and reflects that feeling with more variety and colour than any other—the ballad. Rediscovered in eighteenth-century England and won for Germany by means of Bürger's *Lenore*, it quickly attracted the efforts of the late eighteenth-century song-composers, who, however, despite all their experiments—many of them curious—with strophic melody and with elements of the cantata, failed to hit upon the combination of resources proper to melodrama. That was reserved for CARL LOEWE. When little more than twenty years of age (1818), Loewe discovered with one miraculous stroke the true form of the musical ballad, rendering it capable of rich variety and descriptiveness without abandoning the ground of simple strophic construction. He had not Schubert's universality, although he also composed orchestral works, operas, and especially oratorios. If Schubert's music sprang from the soul of the people and yet was able to achieve the highest and most individual expression, Loewe's was rather for the people—often indeed merely for the public—and was not great enough to rise above an operatic kind of melody and a mere fanciful descriptiveness. But in the realm of lyric poetry he helped a certain romantic tendency, which we shall meet with again in opera, to find its particular expression—the tendency towards gruesomeness and an interest in the spirit-world, as well as the cult of Catholic mysticism and legend. No picture of the romantic movement would be quite complete without him.

If Schubert is the romantic classic, MENDELSSOHN is the romantic classicist. The romantic is, in Mendelssohn, the better part. Posterity has to thank it for his imperishable music to Shakspere's *Midsummer Night's Dream*, for his elegiac tone-p..... is the form of concert overtures—above all, *The Hebrides*—and his setting of Goethe's *Die erste Walpurgisnacht*, his finest choral work; for the elfin, scurrying scherzos of his chamber music, and for part-songs that wonderfully embody the feeling for nature and the tender longings of romanticism. His classicism was the product partly of his natural harmonic disposition, partly of his education, which was more comprehensive than that of the great musicians before him and of a different kind. He was a master of form. He had no inner forces to curb, for real conflict was lacking in his life as in his art. The melodic idioms in which his feeling was expressed have been imitated too much and therefore cheapened. But his instrumental and vocal works alike are masterpieces of refinement, lightness, clarity, and control.

Moreover, in Mendelssohn there appeared for the first time in romantic music the material elements of earlier music—historical re-creation. Just as romanticism in literature and in the pictorial and plastic arts rediscovered the Middle Ages, so in music it steeped itself in the mysterious art of Palestrina. It was Mendelssohn himself who brought Bach's *St. Matthew Passion* to life again after a century's sleep. He admitted into his music the powerful simplicity and the contrapuntal style of Handel and Bach—without, it must be said, being able to assimilate it. He had to suffer it as a foreign element in his musical language, as, too, he merely adopted Beethoven's sonata form, without replenishing or renewing it. Similarly his two chief works, *St. Paul* and *Elijah*, remain in style and intention the witness of a compromise. Yet to him belongs the honour of having been the first to face the responsibility that music's great past imposed—a difficult problem, and one that hardly any serious composer could any longer evade. At this time KARL PROSKE visited Italy to collect the finest of the old Italian Masses and motets as an example to set before the composers of the degenerate sacred music of the age; and a romantic monarch on a Protestant throne, Friedrich Wilhelm IV, took an interest in Catholic music. The eighteenth century had indeed begun to study the works of the past scientifically, but from a merely antiquarian point of view. Modern musicology is to a great extent a child of the romantic movement. It regarded itself in Mendelssohn's time as a servant of art and, full of enthusiasm, turned especially to the supposedly pure a-cappella music of the sixteenth century. Only in its second period did musicology thoroughly justify its existence as an independent science and attempt to shed light on the darkness of the past, to sift material, and by means of reprints to save what was in danger of oblivion. Since then the danger has been that living music might become over-saturated in history. The bond between science and art will only be properly established when, instead of imitation of earlier forms, the principles of the great composers are recognized and from that recognition springs creative art.

While Mendelssohn's extraordinarily early maturity determined his career from the very beginning, it was not until comparatively late and after conflicts and doubt that ROBERT SCHUMANN arrived at music. That may have been a disadvantage for the musician, but it was an immeasurable advantage for the romantic tone-poet. It is a tenet of romanticism that the formal realization of all the arts converges on an invisible centre; and so it was that with the romantic movement there appeared for the first time those dual talents which, if one of them does not preponderate definitely over the other or if they are not, as in Richard Wagner, trained with tremendous energy to a single end, can destroy their possessors. The musician who was nothing more than a musician disappeared with the romantic movement. The fanciful or fantastical standard-bearer of the whole movement in Germany, E. T. A. Hoffmann, was at once painter, musician, and poet. As a poet he gave almost exhaustive expression to the longing and desire not only of the first, naïve romanticism but also of the second, the so-called new, romanticism; while as a musician he had to content himself with imitating Mozart. As a poet, however, his influence on Schumann and Wagner was very great. These two represented, in different directions, the musical fulfilment of what he had foreseen and hoped for.

Schumann began as the youthful champion of romanticism. He found the musical world, shortly after the death of Beethoven and Schubert, whom he worshipped, sunk in the feebleness and self-satisfaction of the Restoration period—in opera, partly in the superficial, sensuous melody of Rossini and his imitators, partly in the unscrupulous "grand" Parisian style; in chamber and concert music, in the empty virtuosity of the Parisian or Viennese schools; in musical criticism, in pedantic formalism. Then he founded, at the age of twenty-five, the *Neue Zeitschrift für Musik*, in which with truly creative and poetical criticism he accorded the great masters of the past their due, and cut a path for all that he discovered that was new, fresh, and original. Thus he introduced

Chopin and Berlioz into Germany as effectually as
he gave vent to his hatred for Meyerbeer's repulsive
operatic humbug. Pianistic virtuosity he defeated with
its own weapons. His earliest and finest works—and
he wrote, until his Op. 23, only for the pianoforte
—present technical problems at least as difficult as
those of the virtuosos; but in his music technique is
the servant of a richly fertile poetic imagination. The
exuberant and rapturous emotional world of Jean
Paul, the fantastical dream-world of E. T. A. Hoffmann, find expression in his "program music." Here is
an alternation and repetition of minute images, woven
out of spirited dance and tender song, hovering
between profound seriousness and pointed robust
humour, between graceful charm and a "smiling
through tears," made one through a mysterious poetical
bond and full of secret allusions. And all this is
clothed in a wonderfully rich and subtle pianoforte
style, which now dissolves the melody in arabesque,
now plunges it into a middle voice, now sets it
dancing on the peak of the figuration or scurrying
through all the voices. It was the new and perfect
form and technique of a new poetic-musical ideal.

From the pianoforte Schumann went on to the
conquest first of the Lied and of chamber music,
then of the orchestra and chorus. There lived in him
not only the subjective disciple of Jean Paul; he felt,
too, an urge towards great art, together with the
romantic consciousness of the duty of cultivating a
connexion between art and the home. If he did not
achieve his object, the insidious illness which had
threatened him already as a youth and which caused
his premature death must be held responsible. Or
did the feeling that he had imposed too great a strain
on his creative powers cripple his imagination? In
each of the fields of music into which he ventured,

his first essay was almost always the most successful. His first songs, in which his exuberant but also
shy and tender nature reveals itself in the characteristic postludes of the accompaniment, are also his
best, and best of all are those in which he was inspired by poetry of so genuinely romantic a nature
as Eichendorff's, or where he gives melodic expression to his own vigorous folksong-like vein. His first
great choral work, *Paradies und Peri*—"an oratorio, not for a prayer-meeting, but for cheerful people"—is his most accomplished. How strong a contrast
this forms to Mendelssohn, to whom he, so much
the freer, the more original and historically more
significant genius, humbly looked up! Only in chamber
music and in symphony could he put beside his
glorious early works others of later years that equalled
them—in the one category the D minor Trio beside
the non-classical string quartets, with their extreme
simplification of form, and the superb pianoforte
quintet; in the other, beside the B flat and D minor
symphonies the *Manfred* music, in which the elective
affinity of two spirits of lofty aspiration brought to
being a work of true genius. Only in opera was he
unfortunate; here another and a greater was to fulfil
the idea of romanticism. And to opera, towards which
not merely musical romanticism but the whole movement was striving, there to find its "redemption," we
must now turn.

Romantic Opera

The material of romantic opera had long been available. In French opéra comique, in opera buffa, in the German Singspiel, and notably in the Singspiel's coarse base-born brother the fairy pantomime (Zauberposse), all its elements were latent. There had been a number of attempts made in the eighteenth century to create a German national opera, for instance by IGNAZ HOLZBAUER on a German historical subject, and by ANTON SCHWEITZER on affecting texts by Wieland, dealing with classical antiquity and mediæval England. The result, however, was little more than Italian opera performed in German. The movement received its vital impetus from the German romantic spirit, which had owed nothing to these experiments, but much to Gluck, to the Mozart of *Don Giovanni* and *Die Zauberflöte*, and to the whole of Beethoven.

What do we mean by the romantic spirit of opera? In the first place it was a question of subject-matter. In spite of the respect felt for Gluck, there set in a revulsion from classical antiquity and with it a growing taste for folklore. Quite a new idea of "wonder" was conceived. In the older opera it had merely meant fantasy and surprise, an opportunity for stage engineers; in romantic opera it became the moving spirit in everything that happened. Legend and superstition provided a world of marvels, filling the air and exerting horrifying or beneficent influences upon human destinies. All nature's secret forces

took on an individual life and were more or less
personified. E. T. A. HOFFMANN was the first in the
field with his opera *Undine*, based on Fouqué's ingenuous, pathetic fairy-tale, and in the demoniacal spirit
Kühleborn created its typical character. Almost
simultaneously LOUIS SPOHR tackled the subject of
Faust and arrested the attention of his contemporaries
particularly with the note he struck in the Witches'
Dance. The actual birth of romantic opera, however,
must be held to date from the creation of a master
musician who by force of a peculiarly sensuous quality
in his melodic style was from the outset something
more than a mere follower of Mozart. I refer to
CARL MARIA VON WEBER and his *Freischütz*.

Hoffmann was right in saying, after the first in-
describably exciting performance of this work in
Berlin in 1821, that since Mozart's time there had
been two outstanding achievements in German opera,
Beethoven's *Fidelio* and this *Freischütz*. Here, in *Der
Freischütz*, the musician's art is no longer merely
draughtsmanship; it is also colouring. Here the German
woodland comes to life with all its magic in the horn
music of the huntsmen's choruses and all its eeriness in
the evocation of the haunted glen; here a born
dramatist breathed abounding life into the girlish
figures of Agatha and Ännchen (the latter a portrait
of the composer's wife), into the weak-willed young
huntsman—a truly tragic figure, this—and, above all,
created with a couple of strokes of genius the character of Casper, "the monster," in Beethoven's words,
"that stands there like a house." But *Der Freischütz*
was in point of form only a Singspiel. Weber had
higher ambitions. *Euryanthe* represents his endeavour
to establish "grand romantic opera," the German
equivalent of opera seria. The worthy Spohr, an
ever enterprising if not always successful innovator.

had anticipated him in this with his noble *Jessonda*;
nevertheless the historic point of departure is the
"programmatic" purpose of *Euryanthe*. That purpose
Weber himself put into words in answer to a proposal
from Breslau for a concert performance of the work.
"*Euryanthe*," he said, "is a dramatic essay, counting
upon the collaboration of all the sister arts for its
effect, and assuredly ineffectual if deprived of their
assistance." And again on an occasion when it was
suggested that the opera might be improved by cuts:
"With so organic a whole as a grand opera must be,
to make excisions is excessively difficult when the
composer has thoroughly thought out his work."

The problem of the unity of opera was Weber's
preoccupation, and the efforts it cost him are obvious
when we compare *Euryanthe* with *Der Freischütz*;
but the result of those efforts was to make plain the
way for the greatest of his successors. Weber employed various means of unification. Recitatives,
linking the formal numbers of the opera, were in
Weber so much enriched in melodiousness, in expressive power, and in the accompanying orchestral
commentary as to undermine the prevailing system
of set pieces. Yet more effective and radical as a
means towards melodic consistency was the use of
recurring musical ideas at dramatically significant
points, in both the vocal and the orchestral parts.
Gluck and Mozart had already employed unifying
basic motifs, in the finer sense of the word, to char-
acterize their personages; Cherubini in *Les Deux
Journées* had made important use of a motif for
associative and evocative effect, and Weber had done
the same thing several times with great subtlety in
Der Freischütz, the finest example occurring in the
Wolf's Glen music, when the hapless marksman shakes
off his last misgivings before committing his mad act,

to the strains from the orchestra of the peasants'
mocking chorus. But in *Euryanthe* this principle was
much more deliberately employed, and with the
psychological penetration of genius. When Emma's
spectral funeral music—already familiar to the audi-
ence from the magnificent overture to the work—
announced in its transformation at the end of the
opera that the sinner is redeemed, the seed was planted
from which, at Wagner's hands, the whole form of
music-drama was to grow. Wagner did more than
perform an act of piety when he began his career at
Dresden with a performance of *Euryanthe*.

The most admirable aspect of the consistency of
Weber's opera, however, lies in its characteristic
colouring. This was a quality with which he endowed each one of his operas. It was derived from
his singular power, typical of the true romantic,
of so handling the orchestra that the individual instruments yielded peculiar and hitherto unknown
effects, while colours were mingled in the most
varied ways. As in *Der Freischütz* the secrecy of
the German woodland and its dark mystery turn
into music, so in *Euryanthe* does the chivalry of
mediæval France, in *Preciosa* the racial traits of the
Spanish gypsy, in *Oberon* the gorgeous fantasy of
the Orient and the fairyland of the West. All turn
to music, which clothes each of these works in a
veil of magical radiancy.

Opera in the Latin Countries

German romantic opera came to birth with Weber's masterpieces, but it was still far from a complete victory even in Germany itself and in the hearts of German opera-composers. "German opera" and "romantic opera"—these are really the same ideas. As things were at the beginning of the nineteenth century, Germanism in opera had to express itself aggressively. Thus *Der Freischütz* was immediately recognized as a counterblast to Spontini, then all-powerful in Berlin, and *Euryanthe* as a rousing summons to the Viennese, sunk as they were in the worship of Rossini. There was nothing of this aggressiveness in the "romantic" opera of Italy and France—a proof of its stronger attachment to tradition, in spite of importations of foreign elements; of the more easy-going way by which it attained its form, and of its internationalism.

In Italy there was a rich aftermath of opera buffa, in which the traditions of the eighteenth century were maintained almost intact. This culminated in Rossini's masterpiece, *Il Barbiere di Siviglia*. Opera seria, however, took on a new shape, and before long the old type of solo opera was no more. An Italianized German, SIMON MAYR, modelling himself on Gluck, Mozart, and Cherubini, was the first to make a move in this direction. His imitators, the most gifted of whom was Saverio Mercadante, proceeded to stereotype his innovations. Externally Italian

opera became richer, but internally even more pov-
erty-stricken, if possible, than before. Instead of the
old string of arias, there appeared a mixture of arias,
choruses, and massed scenes, and showy instrumental
movements. Opera seria now borrowed the ensembles
of its less hidebound sister form, and the two, in fact,
came nearer and nearer in their musical aim. This
aim was simply a more or less subtle or crude appeal
to the senses. The means employed may have been
enriched, but the use made of them was soon as
conventional as before. In opera after opera the chorus
has its regular task, up-stage or down, swearing
vengeance or joining in a "preghiera" in front of
the footlights, and winding up the evening with a
jubilation or a lament, while the orchestra is allotted
insignificant accompaniments or perfunctory marches
and processional music, crude and noisy. It was the
era of the first orgies of the brass ensemble, in
the orchestra, on the stage, and behind the scenes. The
Mannheim crescendo, which in Beethoven's hands
was a mighty means of spiritual expression, became
nothing more in the Italian opera overture than a
fatuously exaggerated stretta. Only the vocal writing
took on more concise and varied forms. The changes
were rung on melting cavatinas and a compressed form
of the da-capo aria. The emotional expression was
concentrated in the vocal line and was enhanced by
elaborate *fioriture*. It was a hey-day of virtuosity
in song. Only a few composers, such as the short-
lived Sicilian BELLINI, with his *Norma* (1831), rose
by finer craftsmanship and a nobler melodic style
above this dead level.

ROSSINI's works represent this type of opera at
its most triumphant. He gained for it world-wide
acceptance by force of his truly magical fount of
melody. The exceptional singers his operas required

—brilliant virtuosos of both sexes, with huge voices —and the business enterprise of impresarios transplanted his work first to Vienna and at length to that centre which ever since Gluck's time had been the principal market for opera in all Europe and the attraction of all composers, Paris. In Paris the new conception of the "operatic" was finally determined; not in the form of the Parisians' own national opera, the amiable "conversation opera" of BOIELDIEU and AUBER, which with its wit and elegance was as unromantic as possible, while not disdaining a tinge of romantic colour—not there, but in the international "grand opera," the first example of which was Auber's *La Muette de Portici* (1828). Within the next few years appeared the works in which grand opera was wholly realized—Rossini's *Guillaume Tell*, Meyerbeer's *Robert le Diable*, Halévy's *La Juive*, and Meyerbeer's *Les Huguenots*. What it demanded were striking subjects, handsome historical costumes, and sensational situations; it showed no conception of an organic scheme, but only a variety of such situations in a monstrous five-act frame. It required the most arresting melodic invention, but relegated the inspirations of genius to an arbitrary and therefore inartistic whole. It is these "effects without causes" that render Meyerbeer's operas, in particular, such detestable examples of irresponsibility and lack of taste.

In GIUSEPPE VERDI arose the musician whose long life's work was to transcend, though in a very different way from Wagner's, the false romanticism of the Franco-Italian lyric stage and the pretensions of "grand opera." He began rather in the manner of the minor opera-composers who won successes in Rossini's wake, especially Donizetti, but from the very outset was distinguished from these by his predilection for fierce and fiery subjects, the simplicity and energy of his melody, his native truthfulness, and the striking conciseness of his utterance. His ardent nationalism found its most enthusiastic expression in his choruses, which render his earlier works veritable Italian folk-operas. With the works of his middle period—*Rigoletto, Il Trovatore, La Traviata*—his fame became universal, purchased to some extent, it is true, by a more pronounced leaning towards Parisian opera. The great Verdi emerged in the last three works, *Aida, Otello,* and *Falstaff*. Here that forceful melody of his, always so immediately telling, and his impetuous scenic art were rid of all dross and were directed to their purpose with utter integrity.

Intellectually and musically Verdi stands as Wagner's antithesis. The vast background—not ground, but world—of Wagner's works has no equivalent in Verdi. With him human beings, tragic or humorous, take the centre of the stage, and consequently the relation between voices and orchestra in his opera is totally opposed to that found in Wagner. Verdi's vocal line is the vehicle of the expression, his orchestra is a background. The result is the immediate and irresistible triumph of his melody and of Latin humanism, as opposed to the symbolically produced impression made by the typically romantic relation between voices and orchestra. What, when all is said and done, is decisive is Verdi's grandeur as an artist, maintained indefectibly throughout his best works and not to be judged absent even from the weakest of them, however stern the criterion; his sincerity, his integrity as man and artist, his love of simplicity, his consciousness that simplicity spells strength. The best thing in French opera after Meyerbeer—Bizet's *Carmen*, with its vivid Spanish colouring and its lively Spanish rhythms and melodies—fol-

lowed directly in Verdi's footsteps. Everything the
Italian opera-composers did after him he had foreshadowed. Puccini's *Tosca* had been anticipated by
Luisa Miller, *La Bohème* by *La Traviata*. As for the
operas of the "verists," they really derive from grand
opera, in spite of the apparent break-up of the old
formulas; for here, too, the success depends not upon
a whole but upon an arresting part—some melodic
explosion, some material effects; in short, upon some
by-product of opera. The successors of Verdian
opera are little works, of no significance in the
historic tale, for their composers were little men.

The New Romanticism

None of the composers of German romantic opera
who immediately followed Weber inherited his universality, and it is remarkable that not one made an
attempt to pursue and extend the path indicated by
Euryanthe. Kreutzer, Lortzing, and Marschner—these
three all represent a mingling of the same elements in
different proportions. Kreutzer, the eldest of them
and the feeblest, had no particular dramatic pretensions, being content to rely on the effect of romantic
German melodiousness. Towards the end of his all too
short and troubled life LORTZING took a more ambitious
line with a romantic opera in which he returned
to the material of its exemplar, E. T. A. Hoffmann's
Undine. His real importance, however, rests in his
popular, or rather middle-class comic operas of a
type which, schooled as he was in the more refined

methods of French opéra comique, he raised from
the dead level of the Viennese popular spectacle and
fairy pantomime, not without lapses into sentimentality and banality, yet with an irresistible blend of
humour and feeling and an assured mastery of his
means. Alongside this poet-musician Nicolai, who
sailed his bark in Italian waters, looks insignificant,
in spite of the bid for fame he made by *Die lustigen
Weiber von Windsor* and although in actual musicianship he was Lortzing's superior; and the Frenchified and unprincipled Flotow is even more dwarfed.
The old mingling of tragic and comic personages
characteristic of romantic opera from its springs in
Die Zauberflöte—whence romantic opera principally
flowed in two different streams—was not altogether
renounced by HEINRICH MARSCHNER; but while Lortzing represents the bright and cheerful aspect, Marschner decidedly inclined towards the somber and tragic
side of post-Weber romantic opera. The weird, the
ghostly, the blood-curdling, was his peculiar province.
In his *Vampyr* this makes its effect simply as such;
but in his masterpiece, *Hans Heiling*, the whole
tragic problem of *Lohengrin* is anticipated, and the
"*durchkomponiert*" or freely constructed first scene
of this work shows a great advance beyond the mere
Singspiel or ballad-opera style. Weber's *Euryanthe*
and Marschner's *Hans Heiling* and *Templer und Jüdin*
provided the Wagner of *Der fliegende Holländer* and
Lohengrin with threads for his weaving.

Romantic opera was the realization of the aspira-
tions of the romantic dramatist. What was denied
the literary drama, principally on account of the
intellectual and ironic elements which the poets
introduced into it—not even Eichendorff kept clear
of that—was possible in opera. Richard Wagner's
achievements, his development of romantic opera into

romantic music-drama, were the culmination of romanticism—that romanticism which saw in art the quintessence of life, surveyed the world solely from the artistic angle, and lived the only moments worth living immersed in music. Wagner thus does not belong exclusively to the history of music; Wagner the artist is the incarnation of his age. But before the attempt is made at an appraisal of that portentous figure, a sketch must be given of the two artists who are classed with him as representatives of neo-romanticism—BERLIOZ and LISZT, both of whom were his seniors and were actuated by similar motives.

In spite of all the differences between them, there is a bond of union between the three neo-romantics, and it links them, too, with Schumann. This is the consciousness each felt in his own way of the greatness of Beethoven, and especially the Beethoven of the last period. Gluck and Beethoven inspired the musician in Berlioz; the singular and contradictory romanticist in him took fire from Virgil, Shakspere, Byron, and the Goethe of *Faust*—whom he frankly saw in the light of Latin neo-romanticism. To his inflamed imagination the classical symphony seemed too generalized and ambiguous in meaning; he set out to give it a literal sense by imposing a "program." He represents a revival, in new and modern surroundings, of the old French national tendency to description in music, discovered long before him in lute and harpsichord suites as well as in opera. Thus, five years after Beethoven's Ninth Symphony he wrote his *Symphonie fantastique*, in which music mirrored a poet's love-story in a series of visions of an opium-eater, passionate or elegiac or grotesque; while his *Harold en Italie* was an attempt to give a new programmatic meaning to the old symphonic concerto. The full orchestra was his principal medium; only very occasionally did he handle smaller musical forces, preoccupied as he was with extreme and gigantic aims. And so with his vocal writing; huge choral masses were pressed into the service of his ideas. He forged anew the poetry of *Faust* and *Romeo and Juliet* to his own ends, and monstrous works came forth, half oratorio, half symphony, half lyrical and half dramatic, all blazing with colour. Similarly he took up liturgical texts, the Requiem and the Te Deum, for the purpose of a colossal musical exhibition and show of power. And throughout these works, as likewise in his three operas—the first the glorification of an artist (*Benvenuto Cellini*), then that child of tragic travail *Les Troyens*, and last the merry *Béatrice et Bénédict*, after Shakspere's *Much Ado* —he was the master of instrumentation and orchestral colour, subordinating all other musical means to that effect and entirely guided by it in the workings of his imagination.

But however subtle and new Berlioz's blending of colours may have been, and however fruitful his "programmatic" idea in suggesting individual harmonic, rhythmic, and dynamic audacities, he failed in the main lines of his symphonic composition to solve the problem he had set himself. The development section in the first movement of the *Symphonie fantastique* might have shown him the way. Here was the place where the themes and motifs to which a definite programmatic sense had been ascribed were to go through a series of actual experiences; and this is what Berlioz sets them doing here. But he believed, all the same, that his work, "quite apart from the dramatic (programmatic) intention," might yet afford "a musical interest," and he thereby gives a clue to the half-and-half effect of its form. The "musical music" in the work is weakened by the

programmatic purpose, while the development of
the latter clashes with the strictly musical sonata form
to which he still clung. Instead of matching his 'program" with music of a closely corresponding development, he chose to divide the story he was illustrating
into separate scenes, approximating to the traditional
form of the four-movement symphony. This is all
the more strange since he had created—or at least
applied with a new poetic significance—in the *idée
fixe* of the *Symphonie fantastique* the germ of a possible development of that sort. The flute-melody of
the *Symphonie fantastique* and the viola theme of
Harold en Italie guaranteed him the unity of his
symphonic whole, even though he did not employ these
melodies in the manner of "Leitmotiv," not trans-
forming them, but only transferring them into a succession of different scenes. It was left to Franz Liszt
to take that step in advance of Berlioz, and out of
the program symphony to create the symphonic poem.
So far as originality goes, Liszt was much inferior to
Berlioz, but he surpassed him in taste and intellectual
power. Nothing is more suggestive than to compare
the two in their treatment of the matter of *Faust*.
For Berlioz this was a treasure-trove of romantic
characters and situations, in depicting which he quite
overlooked Goethe. Liszt at least made the attempt to
deal with it in the spirit of the poet, while reducing
it to the simplest terms. His conception was a
thoroughly musical one, the material taking the form
of three characteristic studies—Faust, Gretchen, Meph-
istopheles—while actual dramatic happenings are only
referred to poetically by the introduction of the
"chorus mysticus" at the close of the symphony as
an indication of the basic ideas of tragedy. Similarly
in his *Dante* Symphony he had vision and ingenuity
enough not to be engrossed by the mere descriptive-

ness suggested by the subject. Engaged on such an undertaking as a *Romeo and Juliet*, Liszt would never have surrendered as Berlioz did; he would assuredly have striven to compass the whole drama into some such plastic movement as Beethoven had achieved, in his *Coriolan* Overture.

Liszt's one-movement symphonic poem is more closely related to Beethoven's poetically inspired overtures than to Weber's "program overtures," the charm of which lies principally in their melodiousness and colour. Some may say that his form is all development without any exposition. All the more attention, then, must be paid to the appearance of his themes. Liszt took the principle of unity of motive very seriously—far more thoroughly than Berlioz—and the art shown in his thematic transformations proves what an ingenious "absolute" musician he was. That variety of expression of his, developing from the most economical invention, was to become a resource of prime importance for modern music. But it was the poetic program that enabled Liszt to shape as a musician in this way, and the program gives us the key to his developments. The form of these developments is as various as are his subjects; and whether it is Tasso, whose progress from despair to triumph is related in the development of a Venetian gondolier's declamatory song, or the triumph of Christianity over the hordes of heathendom (suggested by Kaulbach's fresco of *The Battle of the Huns*) which he symbolized by the hymn-tune *Crux fidelis*, or the admirable character-drawing in the much neglected *Hamlet*—all his subjects not only lend themselves naturally to musical treatment but are also, in Goethe's sense, rich in symbolic intention, far surpassing the literal bounds of the "program." Freedom of form, not formlessness, was his aim. The tragedy

of the pioneer was that he seldom achieved that firm
and finished texture of strong musical ideas which
satisfies the musician. We get the impression from
these symphonic poems of an orchestrated version
of the supreme pianist's improvisations. From the
pianoforte they derive the daring of their conception,
but unfortunately the improvisation often entails
crudity in the principal idea and mere transpositions
and repetitions in place of thoroughgoing development and a close-woven fabric. Liszt's free form involves a free interpretation. As characteristic as the
Mannheimers' dynamic gradations are Liszt's fluctuations of tempo. Thus in his *Orpheus* we actually
find the direction: "Crescendo and diminuendo of
rhythm." A tempo ever ebbing and flowing is the
normal thing with him; an abrupt change of speed is
reserved for an exceptional expressive effect.

The same independent spirit is shown in Liszt's
vocal works, alike in his songs—in which he discarded the compact Lied form in favour of a rhap-
sodic though still, as a rule, not formless presentation,
thereby originating the modern song—and in the
most extended forms of accompanied vocal music, the
oratorio and the Mass. He is both the first and almost
the last musician of the nineteenth century who counts
in the history of Catholic church music. Nothing was
so antipathetic to the spirit of the romantic age as the
rationalistic church music of the rococo period and
the "enlightened" generation. The reaction went to
the extreme of decrying all subjective, individual expression—though it was that of the greatest composers, Haydn, Mozart, and Beethoven—and indeed any
kind of instrumentally accompanied liturgical music.
From this "Nazarenism," which saw salvation only in
a return to the pure a-cappella style of the sixteenth
century and idolatrously worshipped the ghost of Pa-

lestrina, Liszt rescued the music of the Church. He understood the spirit of the ancient liturgical art every bit as well as did such composers as Ett and Aiblinger, but his way was not to imitate it but to re-create it as a Catholic believer and artist of his century. The fact was that for a modern man like Liszt the old, simple relationship with the divine world had been lost. It had to be striven for anew and it inspired Liszt to ecstatic expression, except when he stuck fast in what has been called "the historical and æsthetic amateur Christianity of the nineteenth century." Liszt's two festal Masses, his organ Mass, and his *Requiem* are to be understood in this sense, while his Psalms point to his two great confessions as believer and artist—*Die Legende von der heiligen Elisabeth* and his principal work, *Christus*. The fallacy of "Nazarene" composers of church music was exposed by Bruckner and Verdi as well as Liszt. Bruckner is, in his Masses, the direct descendant of the old Austrian instrumental church-music composers, while Verdi was rooted in the traditions of the seventeenth century. Neither found his modern musicianship to stand in the way of his performing irreproachable service to the liturgy, any more than it impaired his Christian faith.

The great virtuoso and the great man that Liszt was also belongs to the history of music. When he was young, virtuosity, which had since Weber's time been on excellent terms with romanticism, was at its heyday. Paganini represented virtuosity pure and simple; Liszt, Chopin, and Schumann, each in his own way, transcended it. Liszt did so both by the extent to which, especially in his piano-forte concertos and studies, he rose above the ordinary level of Louis-Philippe drawing-rooms and concert halls, and by the high conception he had of the executive artist's mission as servant and prophet of the creative musician.

It was characteristic of Liszt the man that he always subordinated his own artistic interests to those of others. Though never adequately realized as such, he was the father of the subtle harmonic conception of modern music, and he stood sponsor to almost everything that was great and new in the music of his time. His historical significance cannot be exaggerated. As for his artistic position, opinions will vary with the veering of the vogue between intellectualism and romanticism, and according as stress is laid upon intention or obvious realization.

Wagner

Just as Schubert is not conceivable as the supreme master of the Lied without, on the one hand, the floodtide of German lyricism and romantic poetry that culminated in Goethe and, on the other, the influence of Beethoven as an older contemporary, so there went to the making of Richard Wagner a mighty stream of cultural and artistic elements. Classical drama and the subject-matter of mediæval poetry, so dear to the romanticists, and at the same time the heritage of third-period Beethoven, romantic opera, and the achievements of his contemporaries Berlioz and Liszt—all this was grist to Wagner's mill, all this, with enormous energy and consistency, wonderfully assimilating and adapting, he pressed into the service of one purpose, the creation of romantic music-drama, the idea of a work of art all-embracing. For all Wagner's greatness as a musician, the misunderstandings his purpose was to encounter arose from the fact that he was considered and judged solely as a composer. But this poet and musician in one person was, in a yet greater degree even than Beethoven, a prophet. He made use of drama and music as means to an end, believing them to have been so ordained. The different arts which, after their integration in Greek tragedy, had separated to pursue individual careers, found themselves once more reunited in his music-drama. Quite mistakenly he believed the literary, spoken drama equally with "absolute" music to have been superseded by his new synthesis. Wagner felt himself an artist with a mission; drama was in his very bones, it had to become music-drama because music was for him the supremely "redemptive" art, incomparably powerful and inspiring.

The dramatist in Wagner matured before the musician. As a boy he began with dramatic poems and then, wishing to provide music for them, felt the need of acquiring sound technical foundations. This he did easily enough. A few instrumental works of his pupilage, the chief of them a Symphony in C, show his facility in handling the apparatus of music and his skill in obtaining effects. At the age of twenty he wrote his first "romantic opera," *Die Feen*, rather in Marschner's style; then a "grand comic opera," *Das Liebesverbot*, in which he "took not the slightest pains to avoid French and Italian reminiscences." In its tendencies this is a musical document of the "Young Germany" movement, deliberately conscious beyond anything else we possess in the operatic literature of that age. Finally came a grand historical opera in five acts, *Rienzi*, in which Wagner employed all the operatic resources of the century, from Spontini to Meyerbeer, intensifying them to the uttermost. It is as though he had felt compelled to go through a schooling as a composer of romantic opera; he graduated well, proving himself an exceptional student. Already in *Die Feen* an essential characteristic of the later Wagner is foretold in the "redemption" of the dénouement; and in all three of these works of his youth the telling use of allusive motifs shows him already much occupied with the problem of unity in opera. *Rienzi*, with its extraordinary deployment of musical forces, no doubt testifies to the attractions of grand opera; yet, however operatically, a truly tragic conflict rends the hero's breast and is represented in the action with irresistible spirit.

Nevertheless, a turning-point had sooner or later to be reached, and it came with the first unimpeachably Wagnerian work, *Der fliegende Holländer*. The *Holländer* is still an opera of set numbers; it is not without certain remains left over from the operatic past. But what dramatic and musical inspiration there is in the Flying Dutchman's great scene, in the construction of the second act, and in the antiphonal choruses of the third! What a musical unity, this great "dramatic ballad" that springs from the germ of Senta's song! A whole world developed from the impulse Wagner had received from Emmy's ballad in Marschner's *Vampyr*. The sea is the background of the work, and so powerfully is this realized that a prejudiced adversary of Wagner's had to acknowledge frankly that in every page of the score one felt the wind blowing in one's face. And in the immensely deepened and intensified part played by the orchestra—most beautifully shown in the recognition scene between Senta and the Dutchman, and in Erik's story of his dream—there is already more than a hint that Wagner was on a fair way to arrive at a new synthesis of drama and music. His intellectual power and range were to enable him more and more fully to realize this role of the symphonic orchestra.

Wagner's two other works of this period—*Tann-häuser*, called simply an "Action in three acts," and the "romantic opera" *Lohengrin*—represent further stages in the evolution of music-drama out of opera. Wagner at this time was still considering plans for historical operas, but the conceptions he actually worked out were only these two "ballads"—the legend of Tannhäuser, which he most ingeniously linked up with the saga of the minstrels' contest on the Wartburg, and the saga of Lohengrin. It grew upon him that for music—the pure utterance of feeling—the proper material could only be the timeless, the purely human. The human element in the first two works of this period is the redemption of sinful man by self-sacrificing woman, devotedly true, renunciatory, and divinely pure; in the third it is the tragic disillusionment of a lonely divinity in quest of love.

From *Tannhäuser* onwards Wagner composed no longer by numbers, but by scenes. Self-contained melody was more and more dissolved in a flowing, expressive melos (not that even the later Wagner avoided strict melody, when it was dramatically justified). Out of small units grows the great whole of scenes, acts, the work entire. While the drama of *Tannhäuser*, with the fluctuations of the deep erotic conflict in the hero's breast, surpasses the *Holländer* —it may be said to be the work in which Wagner released himself from his own *Liebesverbot*—*Lohengrin* in its musical expression represents the supreme fulfilment of romantic art. The hitherto unknown brilliance and richness of his orchestra, obtained by novel division and blending of the strings and wind instruments, his choruses (so often the weakness of a dramatic work), as also the scenes filled with purely decorative music—all these are signs of rapturous musical creativeness, announcing that Wagner the musician had caught up with the dramatist and now stood upon the same height.

The period of Wagner's exile began with six years in which the creative artist was silent. This long fallow-time may be compared with the period in Schiller's life which the poet spent in æsthetic and historical studies, to emerge at length as Goethe's peer. During this time Wagner became acquainted with Schopenhauer's works, which presented to him in philosophical form the thoughts he had already in part expressed as an artist or was soon to express. He also learned to know Liszt's symphonic compositions and derived a far-reaching stimulus from their harmonic subtleties. This stimulus has been underrated by some, and indeed denied. On the other hand, it has sometimes been exaggerated. Wagner seized upon its elements with such a compelling power as to render his harmonic style after *Lohengrin* in itself an original and independent creative achievement. His chromaticism has virtually nothing in common with the commonplace chromaticism of Spohr.

It was the period of his theoretical prose works, in the writing of which he envisaged clearly his ultimate goal and developed from the composer who had achieved the consummation of romantic opera into the creator of the "complete art-work," which was to be represented by his masterpieces, *Der Ring des Nibelungen*, *Tristan und Isolde*, *Die Meistersinger von Nürnberg*, and *Parsifal*. Farreaching though they are and subtle the æsthetic observation they contain, these writings were really written *pro domo*, with all the violence and the contradictions naturally involved in the foundation and defense of an intensely personal artistic creation. But just as Wagner's creative power was ever greater than his æsthetic understanding, so is his work ever greater than his theory. Now, as once before in the case of Mozart, though under vastly different conditions, there again came into being a musical drama in which a balance was struck between the several forces.

In the older opera the dramatic and lyrical constituents had been separated, the former being allotted the "half-music" of recitative as its means of expression, while "full music" was reserved for points of lyrical suspension in the action. Wagner distributed the elements so that musical expansion and dramatic movement proceeded side by side. The secret of this fusing lies in the relationship established by Wagner between the "speech-song" of his dramatic personages and his symphonic orchestra—"the greatest artistic achievement of our age," as he himself called it. The hundred-tongued polyphonic orchestra reveals the inner motives of the actors in the traffic on the stage above it; it utters their secret thoughts, and the things they know not are disclosed to us. The love that is to entangle Siegmund and Sieglinde is betrayed to us from the moment each sets eyes on the other; long before Sieglinde tells us, we know who the stranger was who had buried the sword in the ash-tree's trunk; we have seen into the souls of Isolde and Tristan before ever the potion looses their tongues. The relation of this "sounding silence" to the visible action in Wagner's art is truly that of the inner will to outer phenomena in Schopenhauer's world of individuation.

Wagner himself declared the art of transition to be the finest and most profound that he possessed. "To be understood," he said, "is of such essential importance. . . . This understanding is only to be attained through the most definite and compelling 'motivation' of the transitions, and the whole of my artistic work consists in bringing out through this 'motivation' the necessary spontaneous emotional mood." This art of transition reposes upon the fundamental application of the so-called "Leitmotiv," which was the old reminiscent motif intensified and strengthened. It guaranteed Wagner the unity of his drama and, indeed, of his whole tetralogy. On it depends the profundity of the effect produced by Wagnerian drama, as also the breadth of the design; for these motifs, of so wonderfully pregnant an invention and containing in themselves endless possibilities of development, undergo in the course of the drama an intense condensation, acquiring a powerful emotional content and a symbolic significance which enables Wagner to unite "the utmost capacity for combination" with the utmost clarity of meaning. The attainment of this clarity required extreme care in introduction and exposition, and the very gradual charging of each motif with its expressive power. All the time the great dramatist never wrote symphonic music for its own sake, but always maintained the closest relationship between the glorious orchestral organ of his creation and the drama, while achieving musical effects of the utmost profundity. It is enough to mention the prelude to the third act of *Die Meistersinger*, where in sixty bars the whole of the Hans Sachs drama is concentrated in an irresistible piece of musical psychology, supreme in its beauty and lucidity. Not "the wealth of combinations," but the spirit of these compositions, their depth and their humanity, make of them the great works that they are.

The role played by the orchestra provided Wagner with the means of representing in idealized form the action of his dramas. "To concentrate everything into three principal situations, intensely compact and powerful, in such a way that the matter in all its depth and complexity stands out clearly and

comprehensively"—in these words he once defined
a principle of his art. But in practice this was not
quite how his dramatic poems were planned and
executed. His characteristic narrations and recapitula-
tions—Isolde's tale of the wounded Tristan, Wotan's
great scene in the second act of *Die Walküre*, the
scene of the riddles with Mime and that of the
conjuration of Erda in *Siegfried*, and Gurnemanz's
legendary discourse in *Parsifal*—all serve the music
in its task of revealing and deepening the inwardness
of the action, and are essential to the whole.

The language of Wagner's verse, too, underwent
modifications with this new relation between drama
and music. Down to the time of *Lohengrin* the poet
was still wedded to a conventional literary diction
which imposed at times a certain languishing movement upon the music, but now he found in a crisp
and characteristic alliterative verse a flexible vehicle
for the new melodious recitative. Not that he was
bound by a theory on this point—or at any rate by
no theory more rigid than that each artistic problem
should receive its appropriate solution—and so in
Tristan we find a free alternation between alliterative
and rhymed verse, humorous doggerel in *Die Meistersinger*, and then in *Parsifal* a return to a more stately
versification. And so also, without ever violating dramatic truth, he planned each act to effect a musical
intensification, and it is a source of endless wonder to
consider how variously he achieves his culminations,
how he allows for points of rest, and how, by retard-
ing and recharging, he builds up the gigantic crescendo
of an act, of a drama, and of his dramatic cycle.
Even in his later period it was still Wagner's fortune
to be able, as with his earlier works, to transcend
his own achievements and mount to even higher things.
After the completion of *Das Rheingold*, *Die Walküre*,

and the first two acts of *Siegfried*, a passionate experience in his life opened to him the gates of the wondrous world of *Tristan*, with all its poignant dissonance that heralds the birth of a new era of modern music. Then came *Der Meistersinger* with its new-old polyphony, and an accession of creative power that enabled him gloriously to consummate his tetralogy, not ostensibly only, but also in inward spirit, and then in *Parsifal* to produce the most intense and sublime of his compositions.

It would be idle to attempt here to appraise these four individually. *Der Ring des Nibelungen*, the composition of which was spread over a period of twenty-five years, during which profound changes took place in Wagner's mind, inevitably turned out incommensurable, contradictory, "involuntary," as Wagner himself called it. Only in the course of the shaping of the drama did it occur to him to convert the dramatic hero of the tetralogy, Siegfried, into the spokesman of the ideal hero, Wotan. Yet his feat in welding into a unified whole this cosmic drama of the curse of might redeemed by love, as mirrored in the profound Germanic myth, remains one of the greatest achievements of the human intellect. The peculiar position of *Tristan* is due to the perfect harmony of its three elements, the dramatic, the symphonic, and the metaphysico-symbolic. *Die Meistersinger*, ostensibly a satyric parody of the Wartburg minstrels' contest, is really the counterpart of *Tristan*. The tragic love so wonderfully represented in the one is contrasted in the other with the triumph of humour. With the lovers' comedy in *Die Meistersinger* is admirably entwined a poet's drama, a thing incomparable of its kind, in which Wagner depicts his own place in tradition, the eternal conflict between new inspiration and the conservatism of the schools, and the inevitable filiation between new and old, the music meanwhile exemplifying the creative transformation of old into new.

The enormous concentration that gives the third act of *Tristan* its sublimity should in *Parsifal* have been raised to a still higher degree. Such was Wagner's intention, which, however, in art and melody was rather less than fulfilled. The ageing master's invention failed a little to keep up with the accumulated symbolism. None the less, this last work, too, possesses a full measure of that magic which, more than its philosophy, constitutes the supreme quality of Wagner's art—the magic of the fact that as a whole it never fails to yield something beyond and above the sum of its action and music and of its external and internal drama. Fundamentally it was Wagner the musician who achieved this, and it was the musician in Wagner who conquered the world.

From some of his contemporaries Wagner received unlimited devotion; from the rest incomprehension and hatred—a hatred to which, with the reckless pugnaciousness of his nature, he was always ready to add fuel by word and deed. He early felt the need of segregating his work from the everyday world and its idle pleasures and of providing it with an asylum such as it eventually found in the Bayreuth Festival Theatre. This he did himself, not leaving it to the piety of posterity, and in so doing achieved the greatest personal victory that any artist has ever won.

Brahms and Bruckner

Wagner the dramatist embodied one aspect of German music of the nineteenth century; Johannes Brahms, the "absolute" musician who, despite occasional operatic schemes, was really at the opposite pole from opera, represented another, without which it would have been incomplete. Brahms was as great a contrast to Wagner as he was to Liszt. Wagner often felt that he would have to make a choice between producing his existing works or composing new ones. Further activity seemed to him at times "sufficient in itself to consume the highest degree of vital energy." That he finally achieved both was the triumph of his unique vitality, and he was driven to it less by outward compulsion, as he himself imagined, than by an inner necessity of his nature. Brahms was not masterful, either as a man or as an artist; but it was the same reserved beauty in his works and in his human relations that attracted people to him, while Wagner, who took his public and his friends by storm and demanded their entire submission, often alienated the most distinguished because they were too individual to be able to submerge themselves in him. One such was PETER CORNELIUS, the sensitive poet and composer of Lieder and choral works, whose *Barbier von Bagdad*, despite a slight influence of Berlioz, is a really original masterpiece, an exquisite blend of lyricism and delicate humour. But in his constant striving after technical perfection in the classical sense, Brahms stands in even stronger opposition to Liszt. His ideals lay in the past, not in the future, and he went farther back into the past than any of the masters who had preceded him. He began as a romantic, and it was as such that Schumann first enthusiastically hailed him; but he very soon felt the need of basing his compositions on a profound study of the old masters. Through Beethoven, Mozart, and Haydn he reached back to Handel and Bach, to Heinrich Schütz, and to the masters of the a-cappella style of the sixteenth and even the fifteenth century. It was as if this late-born Low German felt homesick for the old South German naïveté and serenity; for the paradise of melodic purity out of which sprang his waltzes, his Hungarian dances and gypsy songs, and his folk-song arrangements. His chamber music and songs are saturated with it, and this it was that made Schubert so much the object of his adoration. He based his songs once more on strophic form, as a simple relation between vocal melody and accompaniment, in contrast to the Austrian HUGO WOLF, who transferred the centre of gravity in his songs to the symphonic development of motifs in the accompaniment, although he was too good and, in a restricted sense, too versatile an artist altogether to neglect the stanza. An enthusiastic disciple of Wagner, he placed his art at the service of his poet and in almost every case led up to the climax of his songs by a resolution of one of Wagner's beloved six-four chords. Brahms, on the other hand, drew the inspiration for his choral works, the most important of which is the *German Requiem*, from the sixteenth century. In them he employed an extraordinary wealth of early musical expressive idiom, shaping it successively to his own purpose. The Bible being his highest source of verbal inspiration, he aimed at giving a monumental character to folk-art, and in his last work, the *Vier ernsten Gesänge,* he fully realized his aim.

In his instrumental works, too, he began by an analysis of the past, and his sense of responsibility with regard to form shows itself in his abandoning after a few experiments the grand orchestral form and devoting himself exclusively to chamber music. It was not till the last twenty years of his life that he again approached the bigger medium, in his overtures, concertos, and symphonies. He tried to recapture variation and sonata form for modern art, to realize in his own practice the old ideal of musical construction, to banish everything irrelevant, to fetter but not to banish the imagination, to achieve the utmost concentration of expression, and to develop the thematic material organically and with the greatest possible rhythmic unity. Towards the end of his life Brahms set himself a new task. Technically he had long since reached the same level as his models; for instance, he attains a Mozartian transparency in the Andante of his String Quartet in B flat. In his last masterpieces—in the fourth movement of the E minor Symphony, in the Clarinet Quintet and the clarinet sonatas—he found at last a perfect medium for the expression of his own humanity. But the pessimistic content of these works is no mere personal confession. The master, to whose symphonic ideals Beethoven always remained a stumbling-block, recognized that the age of innocence of the great composers was lost to us for ever. ("How lucky those old giants were; they could let themselves go!") He recognized that neither he nor any of his contemporaries, not even Wagner, were of the streams "down which the nations travel, looking into their depths and at the heavenly sunlight they reflect."

But while the romantic-antiromantic movement which had begun with Mendelssohn and Schumann was again drawing to a close in the work of the classic of the classicists, Brahms, who had infused new life into forms which the romantics had weakened and reduced to mere formalism, there arose in the domain of the symphony another romantic of the first order, Anton Bruckner. A romantic in so far as he made pure sound the basis of his symphonies, and thereby produced his most harmonious work in his Fourth Symphony, which depends almost entirely on beauty of sound; a symphonist also, whose nine symphonies, in contradistinction to those of Brahms (which are really rooted in chamber music), once more attained the monumental stature of true symphony. Of the four sources of his musical expression—Bach, Beethoven, Schubert, Wagner—the Schubertian certainly flows most abundantly in his symphonies. He had the same spring of primal melodic invention, the same breadth of form which, whether in the simple line of his slow movements and scherzos or the somewhat incoherent first and last movements, cannot be traced back to any obvious influence. What chiefly distinguished him from Brahms is the courage with which he again adopts the great Beethovenian adagio form, and his lack of a homogeneous rhythmic sequence in his opening and final movements, which he replaces by a masterly melodic treatment and magnificent instrumentation, nourished by long study of the organ. His symphonies breathe once more a cosmic spirit. Love of nature, piety, humour, and mysticism seek in dance forms and solemn chorales the elements of their expression. The simple, rustic, "uneducated" musician was not a great thinker, but a great and sensitive human being, whose battles had been fought within himself, who had known both

doubt and joy, despair and exultation, and who had
the divine capacity to express what he had suffered
in compositions rich in invention and primitive creative power.

National Music

The attraction felt by the romantic composers of
the nineteenth century for simple humanity, the movement back to the land, the impulse to get below
surface politeness to the roots of things, led to the
development of a side of the art ignored in the classical period: namely, national music. And this brought
into the swim those secondary musical people who had
had no part to play alongside the representatives—
Italian, French, and German—of the universal music
of the eighteenth century. Universal music had long
before flirted with its rival-to-be, borrowing melodic
and rhythmic suggestions; thus, Haydn from Croatian
and Hungarian folk-music, and Beethoven from Russia
in his Op. 59. The early romanticists went farther,
Weber seizing upon melodies from Spanish and Chinese sources, while Slav and Hungarian elements were
fused in Schubert's rhythms, melodies, and harmonies.
Song and dance were quarries for the constructors
of national music, the method being for a fragment
of this raw material to be selected and for the modern
artist to exploit some characteristic feature or another
—archaic melody or harmony, monotonous rhythm,
or primitive-sounding timbre—for his purpose.

On these lines the greatest master of national music,

FRÉDÉRIC CHOPIN, was eminently a modern type of musician. It is significant enough that he migrated to Paris, the hub of civilization. He came before the world as a composer for the pianoforte, and his nocturnes, ballades, studies, scherzos, preludes, rondo, variations, sonatas, and concertos are, as it were, the expression at once of the soul of the instrument and of his own. Every charm of which the instrument was capable he conjured from it; it was never asked for what it had not in its nature to give. Unlike all the great masters of the pianoforte before him and of his time, not even excepting Liszt, he had no unpianistic ideas. This is the clue to his stylistic perfection and also possibly to his intellectual limitations. His age was that of amazing virtuosos, but his own virtuosity was devoted to the service of the most delicate and sensitive taste and poetic feeling. In his melody he rescued the charm and sweetness of the best side of Rossini's melodic style. Over the light-footed rhythms of waltz, polonaise, and mazurka it delighted him to draw tuneful designs of the utmost grace and tenderness and to adventure with them into extreme keys, the darkest and the brightest, through the richest and boldest modulations, while the old alternation of tonic and dominant took on a thousand new charms at his hands. His rhythmic feeling was of amazing sensitiveness, his wealth of figuration and arabesque inexhaustible, and his delicate sense of sound created veritable poems within the tiniest of frames. None of his followers was to succeed in imbuing the elementary material of folk-music with anything like his intensely personal feeling—that peculiarly Chopinesque blend of melancholy and dæmonic passion which can range in one direction to a pathological hypnosis under the spell of sound and in the other to hyperæsthesia.

After Chopin the whole field of music was invaded by nationalism—song, opera, chamber music, and the symphony—the lead of Poland being followed by the self-assertion, successive or simultaneous, of the various Northern peoples, Denmark was represented by GADE, who, adopting Mendelssohn's romantic classicism, tinged it with a faintly Nordic suggestion, and later by CARL NIELSEN; and Norway by the sensitive GRIEG, with his harmonic mannerisms. The Russian school began with GLINKA and included TCHAIKOVSKY—though he, indeed, came to terms with the poor melodic style of German sentimental romanticism—and Finland found a voice in SIBELIUS; England in the noble and sensitive art of ELGAR. None struck so happy a balance between national and universal elements as the Czechs—the lovable SMETANA, who with his temperate use of national idioms recalls Schubert, and ANTONÍN DVOŘÁK, the most inventive and spontaneously musical of all national composers; and then LEOŠ JANÁČEK, the representative of Moravia—in contrast to the many lesser men who emphasized oddity instead of assimilating it, not to speak of more recent musicians who have cultivated exoticism and startling effects for their own sake.

YESTERDAY AND TODAY

AFTER the great victory of romanticism, even before victory was complete, an era of transition set in which, though not yet over, can perhaps be compared to the period of revolution and search for new ways of artistic expression which, around 1600, had put an end to the period of so-called a-cappella music through the "invention" of the opera, the cantata, and new instrumental music. It is the period of the "new" modern music.

The first half of the twentieth century presents a contradictory picture embracing the widest and most irreconcilable contrasts. On the one hand there is the propelling urge towards the new; on the other, the burden of a great and increasingly expanding past. The seventeenth century found it could suddenly speak in two tongues: in the newly acquired language of the "concertante" and monodic and in the traditional language of the Palestrina period. The early twentieth century, however, had the use not only of the language of the preceding generation, of romanticism and late romanticism, but also that of the great Viennese masters, the "classics." And harking back to ever deeper layers of the past, it had, in addition, the language of Bach and Handel, that of Bach having been rediscovered in the nineteenth century.

Music had at no time been more directly the concern of the educated—at the opera house and concert hall—than it was at the turn of the century. The gulf had never been wider between the music of the creative artist and the large mass of the people who sought their musical pleasure no longer at church, in the community, or at home, but through different sources of doubtful quality such as operetta and hit song. Since about 1920 the invention and growth of radio have re-established the link between music and the masses, but have done so on false premises and far more in the direction of breadth than of depth. Since that time music has become as cheap as water piped from a reservoir.

All this multiplicity of effort and the dead weight of an overwhelming past were reflected most clearly in the situation of the opera, which by its very nature is not only the most dualistic and precarious product in the history of music but the most dependent on external conditions. These external conditions belong rather to the field of social history and differ from country to country: there are the nations with home-grown opera—such as Italy, Germany, France, and even Russia—and, distinct from them, those that address themselves to quite different branches and aspects of music and depend almost exclusively on importations from abroad. The internal conditions, on the other hand, can be readily understood when the conflict between drama and music is taken into account —a conflict that must be solved in all operatic works and solved differently in each. Richard Wagner arrived at his solution by working out a new relationship between the dramatic expression of vocal effects and symphonic orchestra while allowing for shifts in emphasis on one or the other according to need: in Act I of *Tristan und Isolde*, for instance, the emphasis is in favour of the drama; in Act II, in favour of the music. After Wagner's death the German stage especially was inundated with a flood of hyper-romantic or "philosophical" operas, full of bombast and pathos, which was opposed by only a small group of independent-minded artists experimenting in a happier and less exacting medium, as Hugo Wolf did in his *Corregidor*. Nor was France—E. Chabrier's *Gwendoline*, for example—entirely free from Wagnerian influence. And however opposed Claude Debussy felt to Wagner, however greatly he abhorred Wagner's pathos and theatricalism and succeeded in effecting a subdued and sublimated coloration in his only opera, *Pelléas et Mélisande*, the relationship between declamation and orchestra is fundamentally no different from what it is in the case of his German predecessor.

On the other side of the Rhine it was Richard Strauss of Munich who established the pure post-Wagnerian type of opera with his more important early operas, such as *Salome* and *Elektra*. This was a type to which, as in *Die Frau ohne Schatten* and *Die ägyptische Helena*, he was to revert later. Then again

in some of his other works he felt impelled to combine
his concept of the symphonic and orchestral with a
lighter, more naturalistic declamation, and in his late
works turned progressively to the buffo, more specifically musical opera. Strauss, of course, for all his
boldness in the sphere of harmony and in the orchestra field, never had anything to do with the New
Music.

This dilemma between "opera" and "drama" is a
predominantly German characteristic. It does not exist
for Italian opera, which can look back to a continuous
tradition of several centuries free of any attempt by
the orchestra to wrest supremacy from the singing
voice. Thus it was possible for Pietro Mascagni and
R. Leoncavallo, and above all for Giacomo Puccini,
to extend Verdi's international renown—Mascagni and
Leoncavallo by their sound one-act works, opera-like
and ostensibly naturalistic in style; Puccini by beguil-
ingly tuneful operas with their overwrought orches-
trations of sophisticatedly brutal texts—among them
an appealing and genuine opera buffa like *Gianni
Schicchi*. Only later, with Francesco Malipiero and
Alfredo Casella, did Italian opera try to arrive at a
purer version of a no less national ideal by drawing
upon earlier exponents.

Another German characteristic is the extreme contrast between the egocentric or esoteric opera of
Arnold Schönberg, which negates the very nature of
this medium—negates, that is, the opera's appeal to
the general public in favour of an appeal to a select
few—and the agitating opera of Kurt Weill, for
example, and Ernst Křenek (*Jonny spielt auf*), which
in such different forms as the sketch, Singspiel, and
even grand opera (Weill's *Bürgschaft*) does cater to
the broad masses. Side by side with this there is a
somewhat more cosmopolitan type of music which

could be called opera of a cult, as in Křenek's *Leben des Orest*, DARIUS MILHAUD's *Christophe Colomb*, or IGOR STRAVINSKY's stage oratorio *Œdipus Rex*, which goes so far as to make use of a libretto in Latin. In order to appreciate however roughly the contradictory and experimental nature of opera during the first half of the twentieth century, one can further cite ALBAN BERG's *Wozzeck*, which in a loose series of scenes combines naturalistic action with the strictest absolute formalism, and PAUL HINDEMITH's various attempts, whether in serious or burlesque vein, to provide a more or less loose link between the action and the music. Finally, there are the numerous regional, national, or nationalistic operatic works in countries big and small, like those of Prokofiev and Shostakovich in Russia (in so far as they are independent works of art and do not conform to the dictates of bureaucracy). This state of affairs is further complicated by the museum-like atmosphere which prevails over the entire opera business, with its continuing cultivation of the old form of opera and the resurrection of still older ones— from Caccini and Monteverdi down to Handel and Gluck—whose production cannot be anything but experimental.

In instrumental, orchestral, and chamber music, just as in opera, there is a schism between the heirs of the immediate past and those newcomers who seek to break with that past. Following his rather Brahmsian or classicist beginning, Richard Strauss continues in his own symphonic compositions the pattern of Franz Liszt, but he does so with incomparably greater wealth of orchestral devices, with a more naturalistic exploitation of the minutiæ of tone-painting, and with greater naïveté. His younger German contemporary MAX REGER, on the other hand, in spite of occasional later lapses into the pictorial, is nearer to taking

over from Brahms. Although he is given to large designs, notably in his orchestral variations with fugue,
the piling up of effects in his harmony and the decline
in his rhythmic devices mark him as a miniature-
painter in music. In fact, what foreshadows the decay of romanticism is the disintegrating equilibrium
between the various elements in music and the emphasis on any one of them—harmony, melody, rhythm
—at the expense of the others.

A symphony- and song-composer of far greater
significance historically, if not as creative artist, is
Strauss's and Reger's slightly older contemporary
GUSTAV MAHLER. His work appears to derive from
Bruckner's monumental symphonies, but as a hyper-
romantic he bases the pace of his symphony not as
Bruckner did on the chorale but on the march and his
melodic expressions on a genre of folk-song, and
enlarges the framework of his symphony by the introduction of vocal episodes or of episodic climax. His
broadest work, the Eighth Symphony, is a great choral
cantata; his happiest, artistically speaking, is *Das Lied
von der Erde*, a symphonic song-cycle. His music,
torn between ecstasy and despair, faithfully reflects
the inner dissonance of the times—the period that led
to the First World War—and in this respect contains
much greater artistic truth than the æsthetic veneer of
Richard Strauss. And his posthumous Ninth Symphony is already on the borderline between late
romanticism and contemporary New Music.

This New Music manifests itself first of all in pronounced hostility to romanticism and to the hegemony
of German music, above all to that of Richard Wagner. Rather than return to the romantic ideal, it prefers
to return to the old models of less passionate pathos
and cultivates a new classical-mindedness. Thus Johann
Sebastian Bach and his seemingly neutral language

appear as a purer model than even Beethoven. As for the struggle against the hegemony of German music: if during the nineteenth century it was only the larger countries in the musical world that emancipated themselves, now even the smallest are following suit, and the larger ones are redoubling their efforts. Even England is waking up after drifting through the nineteenth century in the shadow of Spohr and Mendelssohn, Wagner and Brahms, and is producing a number of specifically British, though not great, composers who, like RALPH VAUGHAN WILLIAMS, draw in part on the rich store of British folklore. In France, the movement away from the sentimental excesses of romanticism is keenest in the impressionism of Claude Debussy, the groundwork in vocal, piano, and chamber music having been laid by delicate GABRIEL FAURÉ. Throwing a veil over the effect evoked by the pictorial technique, this music achieves a new expressiveness through sensitive harmony, tight concentration of chords, free polyphony, and free form. Debussy's "pictorial" phantasy, his renunciation of the rhetorical in favour of a more highly sensitized perceptiveness, have created a new world in the domain of the piano and orchestra. Although it seems to emanate from the surface rather than from within, it represents a most intensely personal kind of expressiveness. With the impressionistic tone poem *Prélude à l'après-midi d'un Faune*, inspired by an eclogue of Stéphane Mallarmé (1892), this new world becomes a reality. The ramifications of Debussy's influence are both national and international in scope: in France itself, the sensitive MAURICE RAVEL is a case in point; in Italy, OTTORINO RESPIGHI and several others; in Spain, MANUEL DE FALLA with his high degree of individuality.

Opposed to these trends is a movement that can be described as international because it ultimately

influences and permeates the direction taken by the
language of music "nationally." It starts out by being emphatically national. The man who must be
regarded as the father of this movement is MODEST
PETROVICH MOUSSORGSKY (1839–81). He was the most
original of those Russian composers who had raised
their banner against "Western" influence—unlike
Anton Rubinstein and Peter Ilyich Tchaikovsky, who
were not entirely impervious to such influence. Moussorgsky's aim was to write music that would be purely
Russian; but this attitude was combined with a dislike
of everything conventional or traditional in method,
expression, and feeling. Striving after immediacy and
truth, he became an expressionist in a new sense, especially in his song-cycles and operas, among which *Boris
Godunov* finally achieved what Glinka and his group
had meant to do and foreseen: a popular opera that
disregarded all conventionality of form and was able
to stir the people by the sincerity and truth of what
it said. In originality Moussorgsky was matched only
by ALEXANDER P. BORODIN, who in his opera, chamber
music, and symphonic works opened up the world
of Asiatic Russia to music; he was surpassed in mastery
of form, artistic attainment, and richness of orchestral
coloring only by A. NIKOLAIEVICH RIMSKY-KORSAKOV,
who in turn became the father of a new generation
of Russian composers.

The international circle that favoured Moussorgsky's independence of tradition and his experimenta-
tion (and to which Claude Debussy also belonged)
includes the two Russians VLADIMIR I. REBIKOV, an
experimenter in musical material, and the "ecstatic"
ALEXANDER N. SCRIABIN, who was bent on an in-
toxicating synthesis of all the arts and who combined his hyper-romanticism with the newness of
his devices, as well as hundreds of composers of

varying stature throughout Western Europe and
indeed the Western Hemisphere. They sought to
expand the range of the musical material as such, to
invent new types of melody and harmony—or non-
harmony—to make renewed use of the whole-tone
scale or to divide the scale according to new proportions into third-tones, quarter-tones, and sixth-
tones; in other words, to replace the traditional
system of harmony, which can be described as a
system with an inherent leading-note quality, by
a system that allowed the introduction of parallels and
combinations. This attempt to give new meaning to
melody, harmony, and part-writing was afterwards
developed systematically into the extremes of freest
"linear" treatment, *i.e.* part-writing which did away
with harmonic interplay—extremes which included
so-called atonality, polytonality, and every other negation of established norms. There is a literary document,
dating from 1906, on this whole school by FERRUCCIO
BUSONI: *Outline of a New Æsthetics in Music* (*Schizzo
di una nuova estetica dell'arte musicale*). Busoni, the
son of an Italian father and a German mother, embraced two cultures and seemed predestined to become
the pioneer fighter for an Italian form of art. Throughout his entire work he attempted an impossible synthesis between Bach-Mozart-Liszt and his own new
orientation. Yet he never repudiated the past and is
important as an exponent of the New Music only in
his capacity as an anti-Wagnerian and anti-romanticist.

Behind all these projects and secret ambitions lies
the desire to return to a more autonomous form of
music and to preclude all possibility of a poetical
interpretation of music. Hence the early period of
the movement is marked by an orientation towards
the abstract which did not, however, exercise an
influence that lasted for long. In instrumental mu-

sic there was a turning away not only from everything "programmatic" but from certain genres altogether. Just as there had briefly been a rejection of
opera and song, so there was now a rejection of
large symphonies and even of symphonic composition: it was the age of the chamber orchestra, and
there were few composers around 1920 who did
not start out by composing a string quartet, which
among the forms of chamber music passed for the
most abstract and spiritual and the least sensuous.

In order to eliminate program music and the element of the "subjective" as far as possible, mechani-
zation was regarded as the ideal of the New Music.
Although all "feeling" in Arnold Schönberg's cycle
Pierrot lunaire for chamber orchestra and voice, which
represents speech-song at a fixed tone level, is invested
in the score, the interpreting artists are enjoined not
to read into their parts one jot more than is in them.
Here Igor Stravinsky's famous formula about the
relationship between the interpreting artist and true,
absolute music applies: the interpreting artist is no
more than the sexton who makes the bell ring; its ring
remains unaffected by the feelings and thoughts of
the one who pulls the rope. Yet Stravinsky of all
people cannot be absolutely held to this view of
æsthetics. His permutations are of immense interest
for all the permutations of the New Music. Beginning
as the most inventive pupil and successor of Rimsky-
Korsakov, he has with his ballet music, from *L'Oiseau
de feu* to *Le Sacre du printemps*, done more to enrich
the whole range of the orchestral palette, from the
most sophisticated to the seemingly most barbaric, than
Richard Strauss or anyone else. But he begins to display
a new attitude to the past in his chamber music,
choral works, and operas, with an inclination towards
what one is tempted to call creative parody which

does not exclude parody properly speaking, ranging from his *Pulcinella* (Pergolesi), *Œdipus Rex* (Carissimi?), the sonata for piano and violin (Bach), to his Mass (Machaut). In one of his most characteristic works, *L'Histoire du soldat*, written during the First World War, he achieves the profoundest effect by a perversion of every musical device.

The German Paul Hindemith, even more than Stravinsky—who as parodist, after all, relates to Tchaikovsky and Rossini—skipped the nineteenth century as it were, preferring to fuse the different elements of modern dance music (jazz) with the seemingly anonymous, "objective" tongue of Bach. Still, in his works that are freest in form the rhythmic elements at least are balanced, and in his later work he reverts increasingly to an expression that is more intensely felt and more personal.

The most consistent and radical composer of the first half of the twentieth century is Arnold Schönberg. At one bound, except perhaps for a few string quartets, he changes over from hyper-romantic (*cf.* his oratorio *Gurrelieder*, the Tristan-like string sextet *Verklärte Nacht*) to unrestrained painter of the psychological moment (*e.g.* in the three pieces for piano, Op. 11, or the five pieces for orchestra, Op. 16). He later compensated for compactness of style by his system of twelve-tone music, which allowed him a return to a consolidation of form and to a more extensive and demonstrable arrangement of the motif and aharmonic aspects of his material, and which has found many devotees or followers. In this combinative or constructural kind of music the negation of emotion is complete. All the same, some of Schönberg's immediate disciples have arrived at a new compromise with tradition—among them Alban Berg (who died prematurely in 1935) in his previously mentioned opera and his violin concerto.

That it is possible to produce New Music without resorting to negation, to program, or to compromise—a music, that is, which is not stamped by the crises of the war-torn twentieth century and its postwar aftermath—can be seen in the work of the Hungarian Béla Bartók (1881–1945). He has his roots in the true—as distinct from the gypsy—folklore of his country, while at the same time retaining his individuality. He restores balance to the different elements in music. He demonstrates that the future of music does not lie in imitation, in parody of the past, or in a vain return to the past, nor in this school or that clique, nor in any particular system, but in the great and creative personality of the individual—that is, in the human.

INDEX

Abaco, 90, 94, 114
Abel, 130
Adam de la Hale, 32
Adam de St. Victor, 18
Agricola, 44–5
Aiblinger, 176
Albert, 83
Aldhelm, 22
Alfonso el Sabio, 30
Allemande, 90–1, 95
Ambrose, St., 15
Antiphon, 14–16
Antonius Romanus, 38
Arabian music, 7–8
Aria, 71–2, 73–4, 103, 106, 114, 116, 132–3, 135–6, 137, 139, 166, 182. *See also* Song
Ariosto, 72
Aristoxenus, 11
Ars nova, 32 ff.
Atonality, 202
Auber, 167
Augustine, St., 17
Aulos, 9, 10, 11

Bach, C. P. E., 123–4, 125
Bach, J. C., 130, 140
Bach, J. S., 48, 52, 62, 68, 70, 74, 92, 94, 97–8, 99, 101, 103–10, 113, 114, 118, 149, 154, 156, 188, 190, 195, 199–200, 204
Ballad, 34, 71, 124–5, 155
Ballet de cour, 79
Balletto, 51, 60
Banchieri, 60
Bartók, 205
Bass viol, *see* Viola da gamba
Bassani, 90
Basso continuo, 67–70, 85–7, 91, 94, 118
Basso ostinato, 70. *See also* Ostinato
Basso seguente, 67
Bateson, 59
Bayreuth, 186
Beethoven, 52, 109, 112, 122–3, 124, 129, 142–52, 153, 157,

158, 161, 162, 171, 174, 175, 177–8, 188, 189, 190, 191, 200
Beggar's Opera, The, 138
Beheim, 32
Bellini, 166
Berg, 198, 204–5
Berlioz, 149, 159, 171–4, 177, 187
Berno von Reichenau, 18
Bertran de Born, 29
Binchois, 40, 41–2
Birds, song of, 4, 52
Bizet, 168
Boccaccio, 34, 36, 72
Boethius, 11, 20
Boieldieu, 167
Borodin, 201
Bourrée, 91
Brahms, 52, 123, 149, 187–90, 198–9
Bruck, 57
Bruckner, 149, 176, 190, 199
Brumel, 44
Bürger, 124, 155
Burgundy, 41, 45
Busoni, 202
Buxtehude, 102, 105, 149
Byrd, 58–9
Byron, 171
Byzantine music, 14, 16, 17

Cabezon, 52
Cascia, 36
Caccini, 66–7, 72, 198
Calvinism, 62
Calzabigi, 115
Cambert, 79–80
Canon, 38, 42, 89, 127
Cantata: church, 62, 74–5, 83, 84, 89, 100, 103–7; secular, 71–4, 88, 110, 125, 155
Canzon francese, 51, 52, 55–6, 84–5, 86–7, 94
Canzone, 89, 92
Canzonetta, 51, 58–9, 61, 64, 110
Capriccio, 86, 89, 102

Carissimi, 73, 110
Carnival song, 64–5
Casella, 197
Cassation, 123
Cassiodorus, 11
Castrato, 115
Cavalieri, 67
Cavalli, 78, 79
Celtic music, 23
Cesti, 73, 78
Chabrier, 196
Chaconne, 88, 97, 108
Chamber music, 71, 81, 86–90, 92–8, 121, 130, 140–2, 156, 158–60, 189–90, 193, 198, 203. *See also* Sonata, String quartet, Suite
Chamber sonata, *see* Sonata
Chanson, 42–5, 51–3, 55, 62, 124
Chanson de geste, 28
Charles VII, 42
Cherubini, 146, 163, 165
Chinese music, 7, 191
Chopin, 159, 176, 192–3
Choral singing, 4, 5, 9, 14–15, 16, 23, 150. *See also* Chorale, Church music, Hymn, Oratorio
Chorale, 61–3, 98–9, 101–4, 107, 190
Chromaticism, 49, 149, 181
Church music, 68, 81, 84, 91, 98–103, 110–12, 156–7, 175. *See also* Cantata, Chorale, Hymn, Magnificat, Mass, Motet, Oratorio, Requiem, Te Deum
Church sonata, *see* Sonata
Claudius, 124
Clavichord, 123
Clementi, 144
Collegia musica, 92
Coloratura, *see* Ornamentation
Compère, 44
Concerto, 56, 108, 123; Concerto grosso, 85, 87, 96–8; **Solo** concerto, 97–8, 140,

145, 171, 189, 192; Vocal concerto, 87
Conductus, 36
Continuo, *see* Basso continuo
Corelli, 90, 94, 96–7, 114
Cornelius, 187
Cornet, 84
Counterpoint, 102, 127, 156. *See also* Polyphony
Couperin, 108
Courante, 90
Croce, 54
Crwth, 23

Da Ponte, 136
Damascus, Pope, 17
Dance, 55, 83, 86, 88, 90–5, 152, 188, 190–2
Dante, 33, 34, 72
Davenant, 80
De la Rue, 44
Debussy, 196, 200, 201
Delphi, 9
Descant, 24
Després, 40, 43–4
Diaphony, 24
Dies iræ, 18
Dithyramb, 9
Donato, 54
Donizetti, 167
Drama: Greek, 9, 75, 111, 178; Liturgical, 28–9; Romantic, 170. *See also* Opera
Dufay, 40–2, 51
Duni, 138
Dunstable, 40, 41, 42
Dürer, 100
Dvořák, 193
Dynamics, 50, 96, 122–3, 172, 175. *See also* Mannheim school

East, 59
Egyptian music, 7, 11
Eichendorff, 160, 170
Elgar, 193
Elizabeth, Queen, 59
English madrigalists, 58–60

Ephrem, St., 15
Equal temperament, 105
Erigena, *see* Johannes Scotus
Erlebach, 92
Estampido, 28
Este family, 65
Ett, 176
Expressionism, 201

Falla, 200
Fantasia, 55, 81, 94, 102
Farmer, 59
Farnaby, 59
Fasch, 92, 114
Fauré, 200
Faux-bourdon, 24, 39
Ferdinand of Aragon, 41
Figured bass, *see* Basso continuo
Finck, 51
Fischer, 92, 105
Florence, 65–7
Florentine school, 65–7, 72, 76, 77, 78, 111
Flotow, 170
Folk-song, 73, 150, 152, 160, 188, 191
Forster, 57
Förster, 92
Fouqué, 162
Francis of Assisi, St., 30
Franco, 26
French Revolution, 142
Frescobaldi, 86
Friedrich Wilhelm IV, 157
Frottola, 45, 48, 65
Fugue, 52, 55, 88, 94, 104, 106, 108–9, 119, 127, 147, 148
Fulda, 41

Gabrieli, A., 54, 56
Gabrieli, G., 54, 56, 59, 84, 100, 102, 104
Gade, 193
Galilei, 66
Gastoldi, 60
Gavotte, 91
Gellert, 124

Gerhardt, 83
German opera, *see* Opera
German song, 56–8, 60–1, 83, 124–5. *See also* Lied
Gesualdo da Venosa, 49
Gibbons, 59, 60
Gigue, 90
Giovanni da Cascia, 36
Giovanni da Prato, 36
Giraldus Cambrensis, 23
Glinka, 193, 201
Gluck, 63, 80, 90, 115–17, 120, 124, 131, 132, 135, 138, 161, 163, 165, 167, 198
Goethe, 109, 124, 139–40, 142, 153, 154, 156, 171, 173, 174, 177
Goldoni, 134
Goudimel, 62
Grandi, 100
Graun, 61
Great Schism, 14
Greek music, 8–12
Greek tragedy, *see* Drama
Gregorian chant, 13–22, 37. *See also* Chorale
Gregory, Pope, 15
Grétry, 138
Grieg, 193
Ground bass, *see* Ostinato
Guarini, 65
Guido d'Arezzo, 20–1
Gutenberg, 45
Gymel, 24

Hagedorn, 124
Halévy, 167
Hammerschmidt, 100
Handel, 61, 74, 90, 97, 109–13, 129, 156, 188, 195, 198
Harmony, 23, 37, 69, 85, 100, 105–7, 118–19, 149, 154, 172, 177, 188, 191–3, 202. *See also* Chromaticism, Modulation
Harpsichord, 55, 90, 94, 105, 108, 118, 123, 125, 171. *See also* Sonata, Suite
Hasler, 56, 61, 62

Hasse, 61, 74, 114
Haydn, 64, 122, 125–30, 140–1,
    144, 146, 175, 188, 191
Herder, 124
Hermann the Lame, 18, 19
Heterophony, 5
Hiller, 124, 138–9
Hilton, 58
Hindemith, 198, 204
Hit song, 195
Hoffmann, 158, 159, 162, 169
Hofhaimer, 57, 58
Hölty, 124
Holzbauer, 161
Homme armé, L', 40
Homophony, 48–9, 58, 63, 104,
    113, 119, 128, 131
Hours, Offices of the, 14, 17
Hucbald, 24
Hymns: Evangelical, 61–2;
    Greek, 9; Gregorian, 15–16.
    See also Chorale, Laudi

Impressionism, 200
Improvisation, 87, 93, 94, 175
Instrumental music, 54–6, 76–7,
    84–98, 101–2, 105–9, 118–24,
    125–9, 137, 140–1, 147, 164,
    166, 189–91, 198–205. See also
    Chamber music, Harpsi-
    chord, Organ, Sonata, Suite,
    Symphony, Viol, Viola da
    gamba, Violin
Intermezzo, 64–5, 133–4, 146
Intrada, 92
Isaak, 44–5, 57
Italian opera, see Opera

Jacopo di Bologna, 36
Jacopone da Todi, 18
Janáček, 193
Japanese music, 7
Javanese music, 7
Jeu-parti, 28
Jewish psalmody, 14–15
Johannes Scotus, 22
John of Bohemia, 34
Jommelli, 74, 114

Jongleur, 29, 30
Josquin, see Després
Jubilus, 17

Kant, 142
Kaulbach, 174
Keiser, 82
Keyboard instruments, see
    Clavichord, Harpsichord,
    Organ, Pianoforte, Sonata,
    Suite
Kithara, 10, 11
Křenek, 198
Kreutzer, 169
Krieger, 83
Kusser, 82, 92

Lai, 28, 34
Landino, 33, 36
Lassus, 42, 48, 52–4
Laude, 30
Legrenzi, 90
Leitmotiv, 173, 183
Leoncavallo, 197
Léonin, 25–6
Lichfield, 59
Lied, 53, 61, 72, 83, 124, 146,
    152–5, 159–60, 175, 177, 188
Liszt, 149, 171, 173–7, 181, 187,
    188, 192, 198
Lobwasser, 62
Locheimer Liederbuch, 44,
    56–7
Loewe, 125, 155–6
Lortzing, 169–70
Lotti, 74
Lübeck, 102
Ludwig, 27
Lulli, 80, 91–2, 97
Lur, 22
Lute, 52, 55, 65, 90, 93, 171
Luther, 61, 106
Lyre, 65

Machaut, 33–4
Madrigal, 35, 45, 48–53, 58–60,
    65–6, 71–2, 76, 110
Magnificat, 102, 107

Mahler, 199
Malipiero, 197
Mannheim school, 121–3, 127, 166, 175
Marenzio, 49, 59, 70
Marschner, 169, 170, 178, 179
Mascagni, 197
Masquerade, 64
Mass, 14, 17, 24, 34, 37–40, 42–5, 61, 66, 75, 107–8, 147, 157, 175–6
Mattheson, 21
Matthison, 153
Maximilian I, 41, 44, 57
Mayr, 165
Mazarin, Cardinal, 79
Medici, Lorenzo de', 51
Medici family, 65
Meistersinger, 31–2
Melody, 4, 10, 19, 63–4, 93, 96, 100, 118–19, 123, 125–8, 131, 136–7, 151–2, 156, 167, 180, 190–3, 202
Mendelssohn, 149, 156–7, 160, 190, 193
Mercadante, 165
Metastasio, 114, 115, 117
Meyerbeer, 159, 167, 168, 178
Milhaud, 198
Minnesänger, 30–1
Minuet, 90, 120
Mocenigo, 38
Modes: Church, 18–19, 21, 57, 102; Greek, 10
Modulation, 21, 89, 146, 154, 192
Monk of Reading, 23
Monk of Salzburg, 31
Monody, see Instrumental music, Song
Monsigny, 138
Monteverdi, 43, 49, 70, 72, 76–7, 78, 82, 99, 100, 198
Morley, 59
Motet, 26–7, 32, 33, 34, 37–9, 42–5, 47–8, 53, 66, 74, 98–9, 100, 102–4, 106, 157
Moussorgsky, 201

Mozarabic chant, 16
Mozart, L., 122
Mozart, W. A., 45, 61, 74, 81, 109, 122, 128, 129, 130–42, 144, 146, 149, 151, 158, 161, 162, 163, 165, 175, 182, 188
Muffat, 92
Müller, 154
Musical criticism, 158–9
Music-printing, 45

Nardini, 114
Nationalism, 168, 191–3, 197, 201
Neapolitan schools, 79, 114, 131, 132
Neefe, 124
Neidhart von Reuenthal, 31
Netherland schools, 23, 40–4, 51
Neumes, 20
"New" music, the, 194–205
Nicolai, 170
Nielsen, 193
Notation: Greek, 11; mediæval, 20–1, 33
Notker, 18
Notre Dame, 24–5
Novalis, 154

Obrecht, 40, 43, 47
Ockeghem, 40, 42–3, 47
Opera, 64–7, 71, 75–83, 114–18, 160–71, 177–87, 193, 195–8; English, 80–1, 138; French, 79–80, 115, 117, 146, 161, 167, 168, 172, 196; German, 81–3, 117–18, 130–9, 146–7, 155, 161–5, 177–87, 196–8; Italian, 64–7, 75–80, 110, 114–15, 120, 133–6, 137, 146, 161, 165–9, 197
Operetta, 195
Oratorio, 67, 71, 100–1, 110–12, 125, 129, 157, 160, 172, 175–6, 198
Organ, 41, 55, 62–3, 101–2, 104–5, 108

Organum, 23–7
Oriental music, 7–8, 9
Ornamentation, 5, 31–2, 35, 37, 56, 63, 65–6, 67, 70, 84–5, 94, 114, 115, 135–6, 166
Orpheus, 8
Ossian, 153
Ostinato, 70, 88, 102
Oswald von Wolkenstein, 31
Overture, 137, 147, 174, 189; French, 92, 114; Venetian, 78, 97. See also Symphony

Pachelbel, 102, 105
Paganini, 176
Palestrina, 52–3, 54, 156, 175–6, 195
Papacy, 32, 35
Partita, 94, 108
Passacaglia, 105. See also Ostinato
Passepied, 90
Passion, settings of the, 43, 100, 107, 156
Pastoral, 71
Pastourelle, 28–9
Paul, Jean, 159
Paumann, 41
Pergolesi, 120, 134, 138, 146
Peri, 67
Pérotin, 25–6
Perrin, 79–80
Persian music, 7–8
Petrarch, 34, 72
Petrucci, 45
Petzel, 91
Philidor, 138
Philippe de Vitry, 33
Philippe le Beau, 45
Philippe le Bon, 42
Pianoforte, 140, 159, 175, 176, 192, 200. See also Chamber music, Sonata
Piccinni, 135
Pierre de la Croix, 33
Pilkington, 59
Plainsong, 14–21. See also Chorale

Polymelody, 26
Polyphony, 5, 22–7, 32–45, 63–4, 65, 66, 70, 81, 85–7, 93–4, 99, 102–3, 105, 108, 127–8, 131
Polytonality, 202
Program music, 9, 35, 52, 89, 159, 171–5. See also Symphonic poem
Prose, 17
Proske, 157
Provenzale, 79
Ptolemæus, 11
Puccini, 169, 197
Pugnani, 114
Purcell, 81
Puschmann, 32
Pythagoras, 8, 11

Quarter-tones, 202
Quodlibet, 57, 60

Radio, 195
Rameau, 115, 118
Ravel, 200
Rebikov, 201
Recitative, 67, 71–2, 103, 104, 106, 114, 117, 139, 163, 182
Reformation, 61
Reger, 198–9
Reichardt, 124–5
Reiche, 91
Reichenau, 19
Reincken, 108
Religion, music and, 4, 8, 13–18, 66, 74–5, 103, 105–8, 110–11, 175–6. See also Church music
Renaissance, 46 ff.
Requiem, 172, 176, 188
Respighi, 200
Responsorial song, 14–16
Rhaw, 62
Rhythm, 4–5, 146, 172, 191–2. See also Dance
Ricercar, 51, 52, 55, 102
Rimsky-Korsakov, 201, 203

Roman music: ancient, 11; mediæval, 15–16; Renaissance, 69, 73, 77–8, 133
Romanticism, 149 ff.
Rondeau: dance, 91; song, 28, 34
Rondo, 120, 192
Rore, 49, 54
Rospigliosi, 77
Rossi, 73
Rossini, 158, 165–7, 192
Rousseau, 22, 113, 125, 139
Russian music, 191, 193, 201

Sachs, 32
St. Gall, 18, 28
St. Martial de Limoges, 28
Sakadas, 9
Sammartini, 120
Sannazaro, 72
Sarabande, 90–1
Savioni, 73
Scales: Greek, 10; mediæval, 18–19; pentatonic, 7, 41; twelve-note, 198
Scarlatti, A., 73–4, 79
Scarlatti, D., 123
Scheibe, 113
Scheidt, 63, 100–1
Schein, 98
Schikaneder, 139
Schiller, 139, 142, 148, 153, 154, 181
Schobert, 130
Schönberg, 197, 203–4
Schopenhauer, 181, 182
Schubart, 124–5
Schubert, 125, 149, 151–6, 158, 177, 188, 190, 193
Schulz, 124
Schumann, 149, 150, 157–60, 176, 188, 190
Schürmann, 82
Schütz, 56, 61, 82, 99–101, 103, 188
Schweitzer, 161
Scriabin, 201
Senfl, 57–8

Sequence, 17, 28
Serenade, 123
Shakspere, 58, 80, 156, 171
Sibelius, 193
Sigismund, Archduke, 44
Silcher, 150
Simpson, 93–4
Sirventes, 28, 30
Sixth-tones, 202
Smetana, 193
Solmization, 20–1
Sonata, 52, 56, 64, 81, 84–96, 118–21, 151–2, 157, 173; orchestral, 84, 95; solo, 93–6, 123, 125–9, 144–5, 148, 192; sonata da camera, 90, 108; sonata da chiesa, 89–90, 91; tower, 91; trio, 81, 87–90, 93
Song, solo, 4, 5, 9, 14, 17, 28–32, 63–83, 146, 150, 152–5, 160, 175, 187–9, 193. See also Aria, Folksong, German song, Lied
Spanish music, 29–30, 52, 168, 191, 200
Spohr, 162–3, 181
Spontini, 117, 178
Squarcialupi, 51
Stabat Mater, 18
Stamitz, 121
Stolberg, 124
Stoltzer, 57
Stradella, 73
Strauss, 196–7, 198, 199, 203
Stravinsky, 198, 203–4
String quartet, 126–9, 140, 145, 147, 148, 152, 189, 203
Suite, 55, 90–2, 105, 108, 120, 171
Sumer is icumen in, 23
Sweelinck, 56, 102
Symphonic poem, 173–5
Symphony, 56, 78, 85, 92, 97, 98, 104, 112, 114, 120–2, 123, 125–30, 141, 143, 145, 147–8, 150–2, 160, 171–4, 178, 189–91, 193
Syrian chant, 14, 15, 16

Tallis, 58
Tartini, 90, 94, 97
Tasso, 65, 72
Tchaikovsky, 193, 201
Te Deum, 81, 172
Telemann, 92
Tenso, 28, 30
Theocritus, 65, 71
Theorists: Greek, 11; Roman, 11, 20; mediæval, 24, 26, 41; Renaissance, 68, 118–19
Thibaut de Champagne, 29
Third-tones, 202
Thirty Years' War, 99
Thomas de Celano, 18
Tinctoris, 41
Toccata, 51, 102, 108
Tomkins, 59, 60
Tonality, 21, 30, 50. See also Atonality, Modes, Scales, Polytonality
Torelli, 97
Traetta, 115
Trent, Council of, 66
Triumphs of Oriana, The, 59
Trope, 16–18, 24–6, 28
Troubadours, 28–9
Trouvères, 28–9
Tuotilo, 18
Twelve-tone music, 204
Tye, 46

Variations, 52, 86, 87–8, 93, 102, 108, 120, 129, 140, 148, 152, 192
Vaughan Williams, 200
Vecchi, 59, 60
Venetian schools, 54–6, 67–8, 73–5, 77–9, 84–5, 133
Venice, 65, 68, 73, 77, 134
Venosa, see Gesualdo
Veracini, 94
Verdi, 167–9, 176, 197
Verists, 169
Viadana, 68
Viennese school, 123, 127, 152, 158. See also Beethoven, Haydn, Mozart, Schubert

Villanella, 51, 53, 60, 110
Viol, 23, 81
Viola da gamba, 52, 87, 93
Violin, 23, 84, 87, 91, 93–8. See also Chamber music, Concerto, Sonata, String quartet
Violoncello, 87, 108
Viotti, 97
Virelai, 34
Virgil, 65, 71, 171
Virginal, 55
Virtuosity, 55, 69, 85–6, 93, 95–7, 114, 140, 158–9, 166–7, 176, 192
Vitali, 90
Vivaldi, 97

Wackenroder, 150
Wagner, 12, 149, 158, 164, 167, 168, 170–1, 177–86, 188, 190, 196, 199–200
Walther, J., 62
Walther von der Vogelweide, 31
Waltramus, 18
Ward, 60
Weber, 149, 150, 162–5, 169, 176, 191
Weelkes, 58, 59
Weill, 197
Weisse, 138
Werckmeister, 105
White, 58
Whole-tone scale, 202
Wieland, 161
Wilbye, 58, 59–60
Willaert, 48–9, 54
Wind instruments, 8–9, 22, 55, 84, 87, 91, 93, 96, 121, 137, 140, 180
Wipo, 18
Wolf, 188, 196
World War, First, 199, 204

Zarlino, 54, 68
Zelter, 124–5
Zeno, 114
Zumsteeg, 125, 153

*ALFRED EINSTEIN, internationally fa-
mous musicologist, was born in Munich,
Germany, in 1880, and died in this country
in 1952. He devoted his entire life to the
study of music, and was not only a brilliant
historian and critic, but an outstanding au-
thority on the music of Mozart and the
Italian madrigal. His books on these subjects
are considered definitive.* A Short History
of Music, *published in Germany in 1920
and in the United States in 1940, has been
hailed as a* tour de force. *Einstein left Germany in 1933 and became an American citi-
zen in 1944. He was Professor of Music at
Smith College from 1939 to 1950.*

VINTAGE HISTORY AND CRITICISM OF
LITERATURE, MUSIC, AND ART

V-418   AUDEN, W. H. *The Dyer's Hand*

V-398   AUDEN, W. H. *The Enchafèd Flood*

V-22   BARZUN, JACQUES *The Energies of Art*

V-93   BENNETT, JOAN *Four Metaphysical Poets*

V-269   BLOTNER & GWYNN (eds.) *Faulkner at the University*

V-259   BUCKLEY, JEROME H. *The Victorian Temper*

V-51   BURKE, KENNETH *The Philosophy of Literary Form*

V-75   CAMUS, ALBERT *The Myth of Sisyphus*

V-171   CRUTTWELL, PATRICK *The Shakespearean Moment*

V-471   DUVEAU, GEORGES *1848: The Making of a Revolution*

V-4   EINSTEIN, ALFRED *A Short History of Music*

V-261   ELLIS-FERMOR, UNA *Jacobean Drama:* An Interpretation

V-177   FULLER, EDMUND *Man in Modern Fiction*

V-13   GILBERT, STUART *James Joyce's Ulysses*

V-363   GOLDWATER, ROBERT *Primitivism in Modern Art*, Revised Edition

V-114   HAUSER, ARNOLD *Social History of Art*, v. I

V-115   HAUSER, ARNOLD *Social History of Art*, v. II

V-116   HAUSER, ARNOLD *Social History of Art*, v. III

V-117   HAUSER, ARNOLD *Social History of Art*, v. IV

V-438   HELLER, ERICH *The Artist's Journey into the Interior and Other Essays*

V-20   HYMAN, S. E. *The Armed Vision*

V-38   HYMAN, S. E. (ed.) *The Critical Performance*

V-41   JAMES, HENRY *The Future of the Novel*

V-12   JARRELL, RANDALL *Poetry and the Age*

V-88   KERMAN, JOSEPH *Opera as Drama*

V-260   KERMODE, FRANK *The Romantic Image*

V-83   KRONENBERGER, LOUIS *Kings and Desperate Men*

V-167   LA ROCHEFOUCAULD *Maxims*

V-90   LEVIN, HARRY *The Power of Blackness*

V-296   MACDONALD, DWIGHT *Against the American Grain*

V-55   MANN, THOMAS *Essays*

V-720   MIRSKY, D. S. *A History of Russian Literature*

V-344   MUCHNIC, HELEN *From Gorky to Pasternak*

V-118   NEWMAN, ERNEST *Great Operas*, Volume I

V-119   NEWMAN, ERNEST *Great Operas*, Volume II

V-107   NEWMAN, ERNEST *Wagner as Man and Artist*

V-383   O'BRIEN, CONOR CRUISE *Writers and Politics*

V-161   PICASSO, PABLO *Picasso & the Human Comedy*

V-372   PRITCHETT, V. S. *The Living Novel and Later Appreciations*

V-24   RANSOM, JOHN CROWE *Poems and Essays*

V-412   SAARINEN, ALINE B. *The Proud Possessors*

V-89   SCHORER, MARK *William Blake*

V-108   SHAHN, BEN *The Shape of Content*

V-275   SHAPIRO, KARL *In Defense of Ignorance*

V-415   SHATTUCK, ROGER *The Banquet Years*, Revised

V-366   SHATTUCK, ROGER *Proust's Binoculars*

V-186   STEINER, GEORGE *Tolstoy or Dostoevsky*

V-278   STEVENS, WALLACE *The Necessary Angel*

V-39   STRAVINSKY, IGOR *The Poetics of Music*

V-100	SULLIVAN, J. W. N. *Beethoven:* His Spiritual Development
V-243	SYPHER, WYLIE (ed.) *Art History:* An Anthology of Modern Criticism
V-266	SYPHER, WYLIE *Loss of the Self*
V-229	SYPHER, WYLIE *Rococo to Cubism*
V-166	SZE, MAI-MAI *The Way of Chinese Painting*
V-179	THOMSON, VIRGIL *Music Reviewed 1940-1954* (Vintage Original)
V-214	THOMSON, VIRGIL *The State of Music*
V-162	TILLYARD, E. M. W. *Elizabethan World Picture*
V-35	TINDALL, WILLIAM YORK *Forces in Modern British Literature*
V-82	TOYE, FRANCIS *Verdi:* His Life and Works
V-62	TURNELL, MARTIN *The Novel in France*
V-194	VALÉRY, PAUL *The Art of Poetry*
V-347	WARREN, ROBERT PENN *Selected Essays*
V-122	WILENSKI, R. H. *Modern French Painters,* Volume I (1863-1903)
V-123	WILENSKI, R. H. *Modern French Painters,* Volume II (1904-1938)
V-218	WILSON, EDMUND *Classics & Commercials*
V-181	WILSON, EDMUND *The Shores of Light*
V-360	WIMSATT & BROOKS *Literary Criticism*

A free catalogue of VINTAGE BOOKS *will be sent at your request. Write to* Vintage Books, 457 Madison Avenue, New York, New York 10022.